A Gustav Klimt Sampler

By

Carl Scott Harker

The front cover features Gustav Klimt's 1903 painting "Farmhouse With Birch Trees." The back cover features a 1908 photo of Gustav Klimt

Copyright Notice

Cover design by Carl Scott Harker

Copyright © 2020 Carl Scott Harker

Note: The artworks presented in this work are in the public domain. This book, as published, is, of course, copyrighted.

An Aldouspi Publication

Table of Contents

Introduction .... Page 5

Landscapes

The Castle With A Moat .... Page 9
The Beech Grove .... Page 10
The Apple Tree .... Page 11
The Sunflower .... Page 12
Church in Cassone .... Page 13
The Cottage Garden .... Page 14
Chickens In Garden .... Page 15
Houses at Unterach on the Attersee .... Page 16
Mountain Slope at Unterach .... Page 17
Large Poplar Tree And Coming Storm .... Page 18
Orchard with Roses .... Page 19
Attersea .... Page 20

People

Portrait of Mada Primavesi .... Page 22
Blind Man .... Page 23
Lady With Fan .... Page 24
The Kiss .... Page 25
Portrait of Adele Bloch Bauer .... Page 26
Portrait of Man With Beard .... Page 27
Portrait of Frieda Reidel .... Page 28
Portrait of Young Woman Reclining .... Page 29
Portrait of an Old Man Wearing an Ivy Wreath .... Page 30
Portrait of a Lady .... Page 31

Woman in White Dress .... Page 32
Portrait of the Artist's Dead Son .... Page 33
Baby Cradle .... Page 34
Portrait of a Woman in an Armchair .... Page 35

Nudes

Eve and Adam .... Page 37
Salomé .... Page 38
The Maiden .... Page 39
Allegory of a Statue .... Page 40
Mother and Child .... Page 41
Two Studies of a Seated Nude with Long Hair .... Page 42
Hope II .... Page 43
Two Friends .... Page 44
Nude Male Sitting .... Page 45
Judith .... Page 46
Danae .... Page 47
Fable .... Page 48
Cold Fish .... Page 49
Death and Life .... Page 50
Nude Rear .... Page 51
Girl With Blue Veil .... Page 52
Suffering of the Weak .... Page 53
The Three Ages of Woman .... Page 54
Female Nude Turned Left .... Page 55
The Dancer .... Page 56

About the Author .... Page 57
Other Books by the Author available on Amazon ... Page 57

Introduction

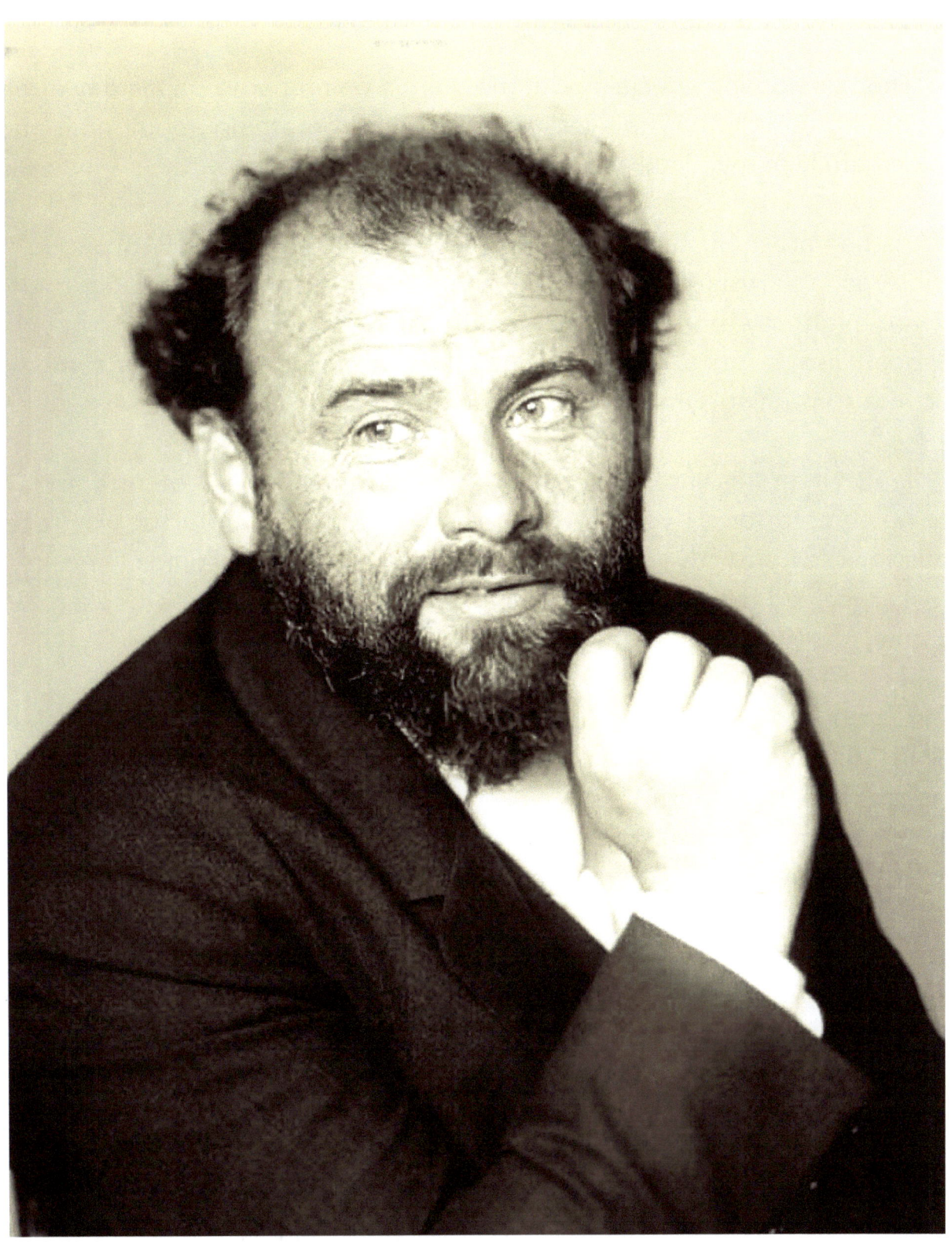

Gustav Klimt, 1908

"I have never painted a self-portrait. I am less interested in myself as a subject for a painting than I am in other people, above all women...

"There is nothing special about me. I am a painter who paints day after day from morning to night... Who ever wants to know something about me... ought to look carefully at my pictures." – Gustav Klimt.

Austrian artist Gustav Klimt (July 14, 1862 - February 6, 1918) is one of the most interesting artists of the late 19th and early 20th century. Looking at his style of art you might say there are touches of realism, impressionism, a nod to Japanism & pointillism, aspects of art nouveau and more. But all of it is so combined as to become something symbolically unique and great.

Klimt, when he was 14, enrolled at the Vienna School of Arts and Crafts where he studied for six years. Within four years, the young artist was receiving commissions for artwork – mainly for interior murals and ceilings. And in 1888, the artist received the Golden Order of Merit in Arts from Emperor Franz Josef I of Austria.

In 1894, the painter, who is most often referred to as the Austrian Symbolist, became a founding member of the Vienna Art Nouveau (Vienna Secession) movement. This organization promoted lesser known artist and arranged for the works of foreign artists to be displayed in Vienna. It was also during the early 1890's, that Klimt met Emilie Flöge, who was to be his companion for the rest of his life.

An interesting moment in the evolution of Klimt's paintings occurred during what is called his "Gold Phase." For a decade, Klimt added gold leaf to many of his paintings, which turned out to be a very successful move for the artist. Two of his Gold Period works are included in this sampler: "The Kiss" and "Portrait of Adele Bloch Bauer."

After the Gold Phase, Klimt's palette became more of a kaleidoscope of colors where the placement of color on the canvas became more important than the form the paint was creating.

After the Gold Phase, Klimt's palette became more of a kaleidoscope of colors where the placement of color on the canvas became more important than the form the paint was creating.

This book provides a selection of what I believe is some of the best of Klimt's artwork. I have divided these paintings and drawings into three categories to best display his talent: Landscapes, People and Nudes. Enjoy!

LANDSCAPES

The Castle With A Moat

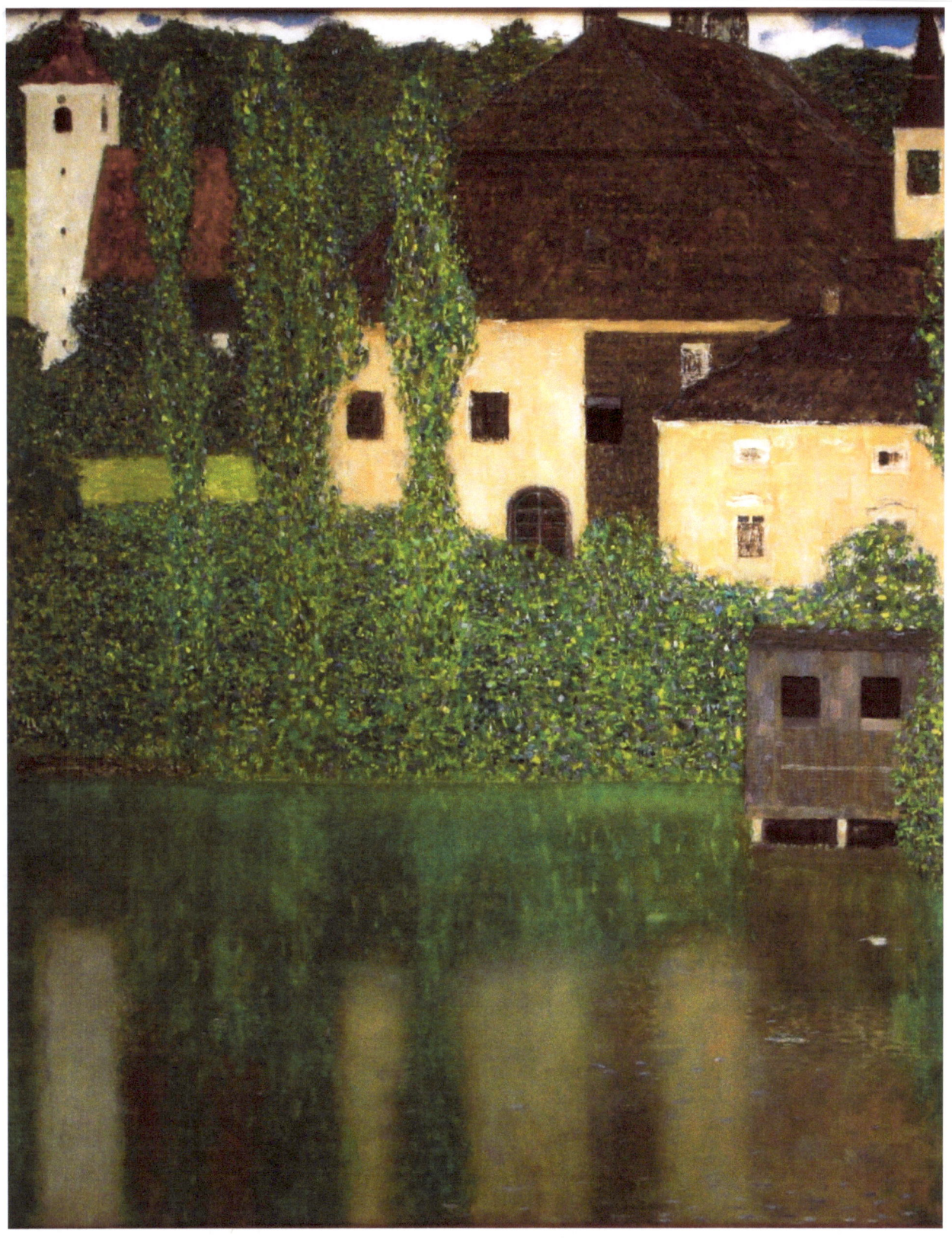

The Beech Grove

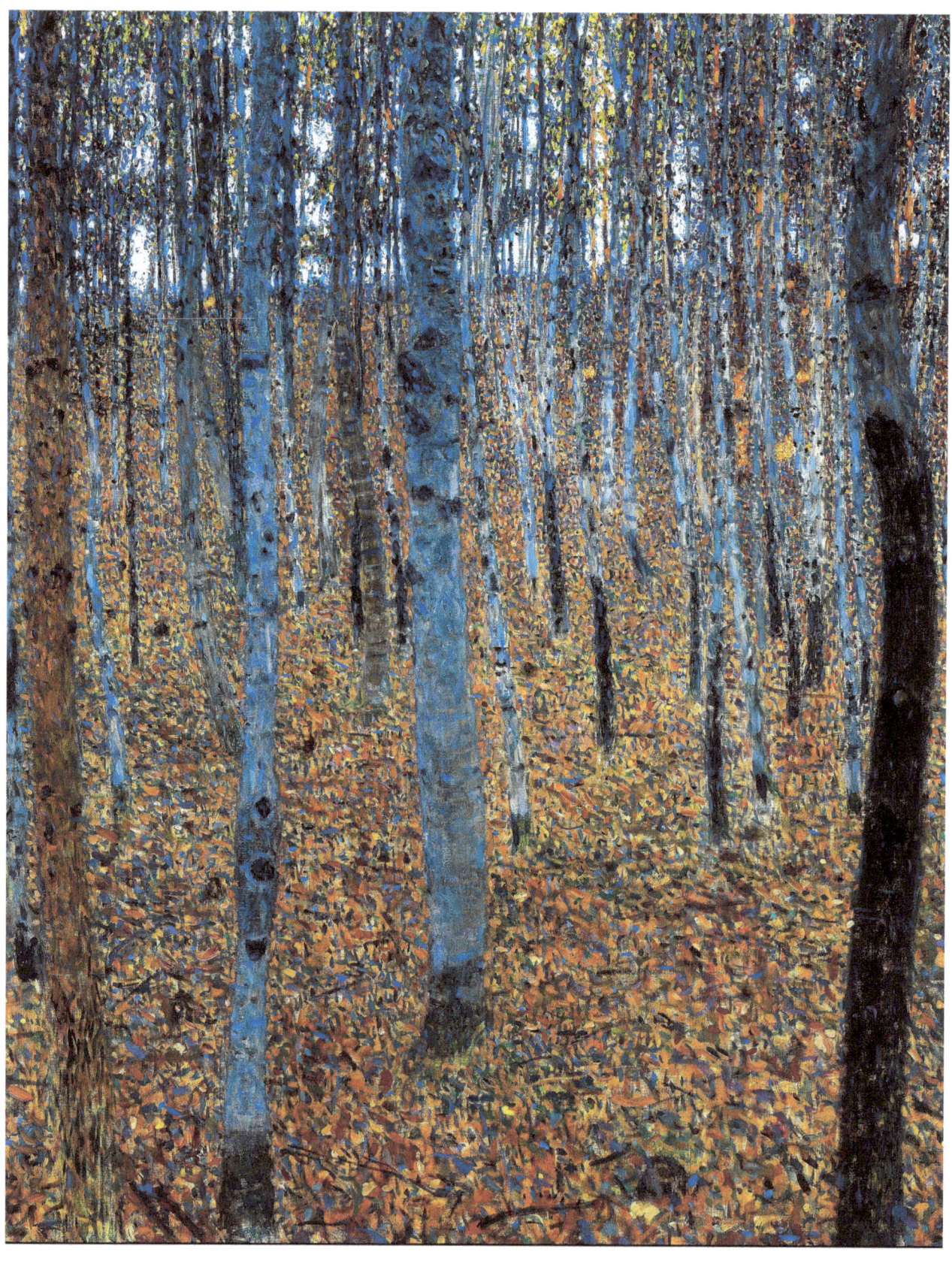

The Apple Tree

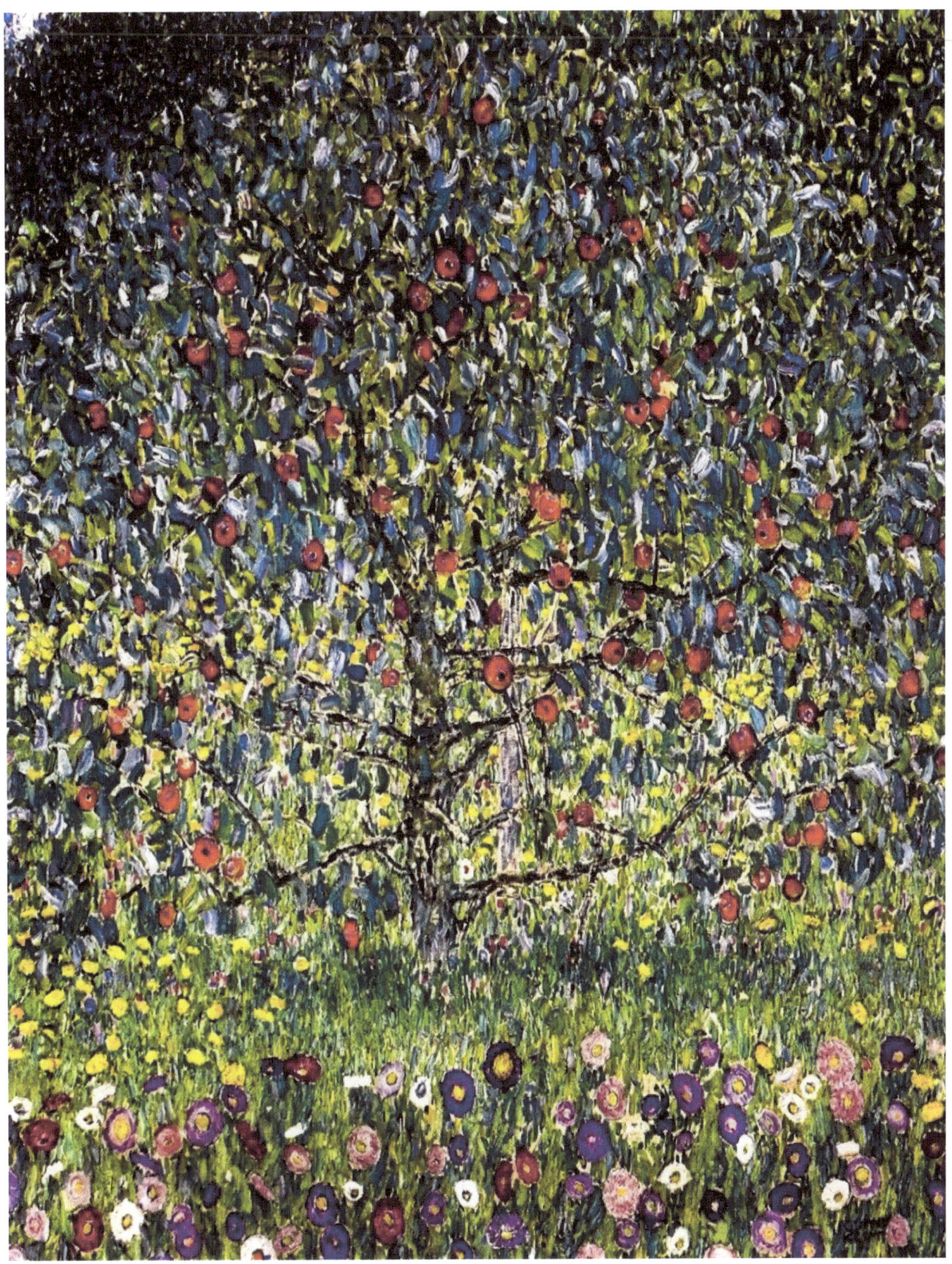

The Sunflower

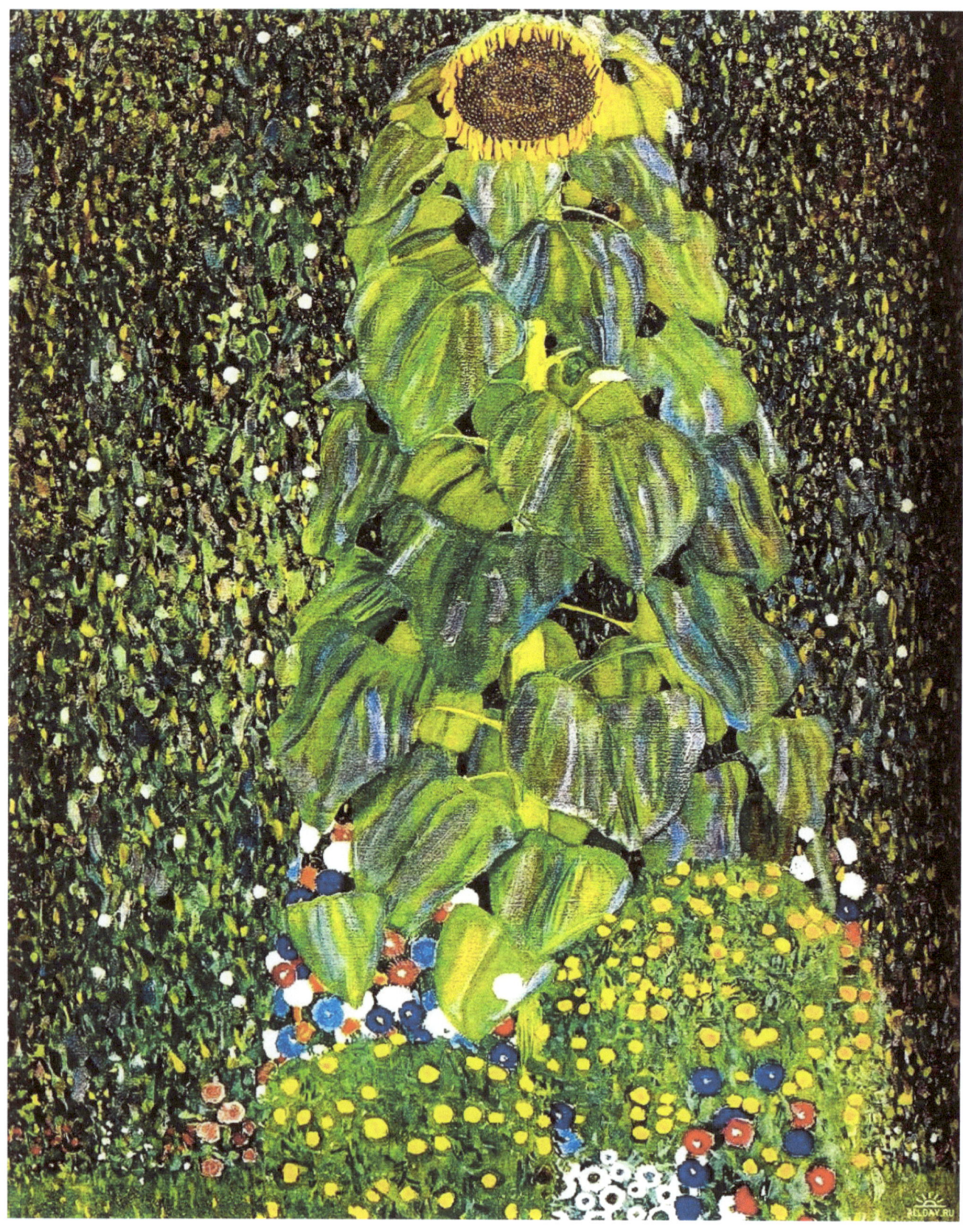

Church in Cassone

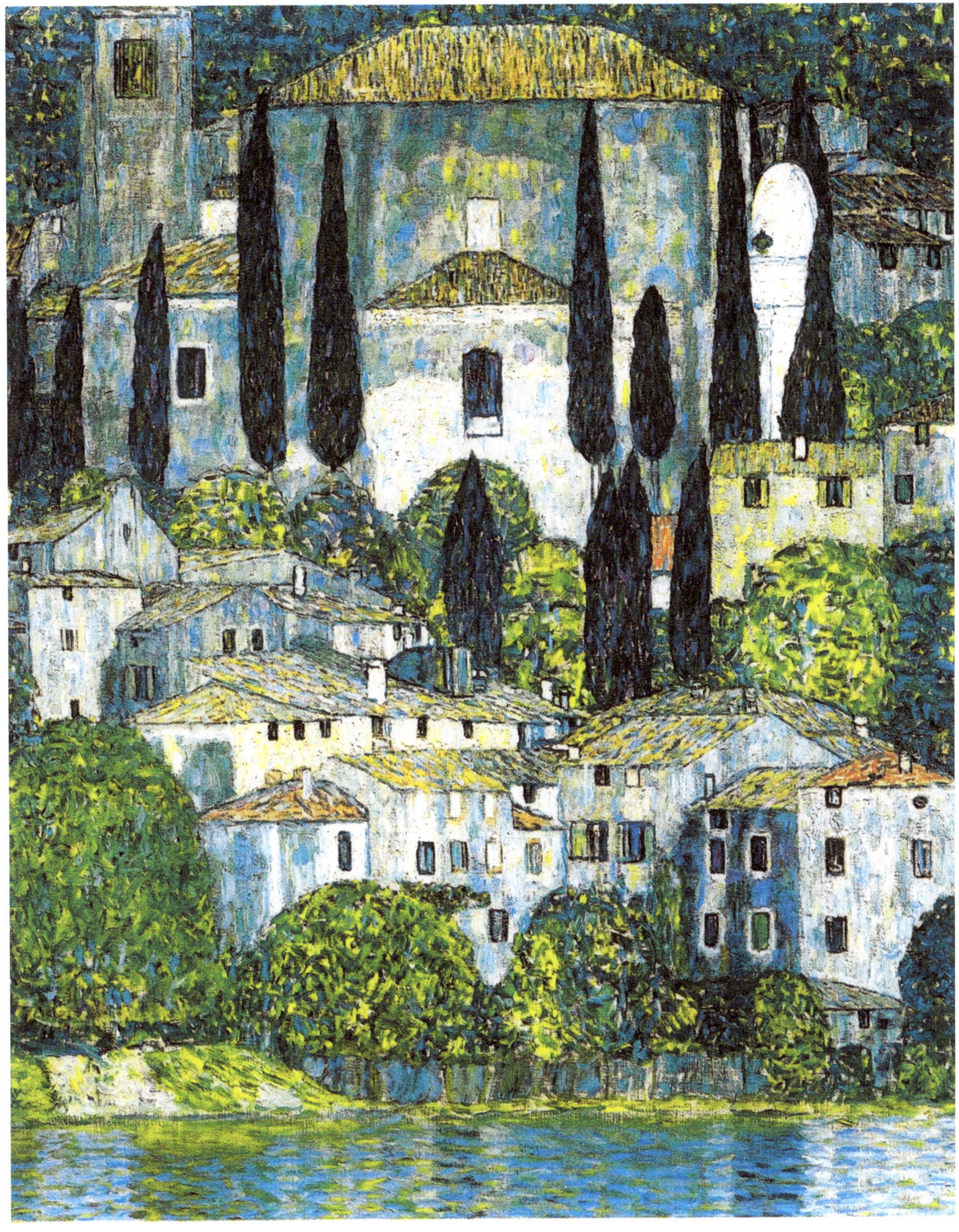

The Cottage Garden

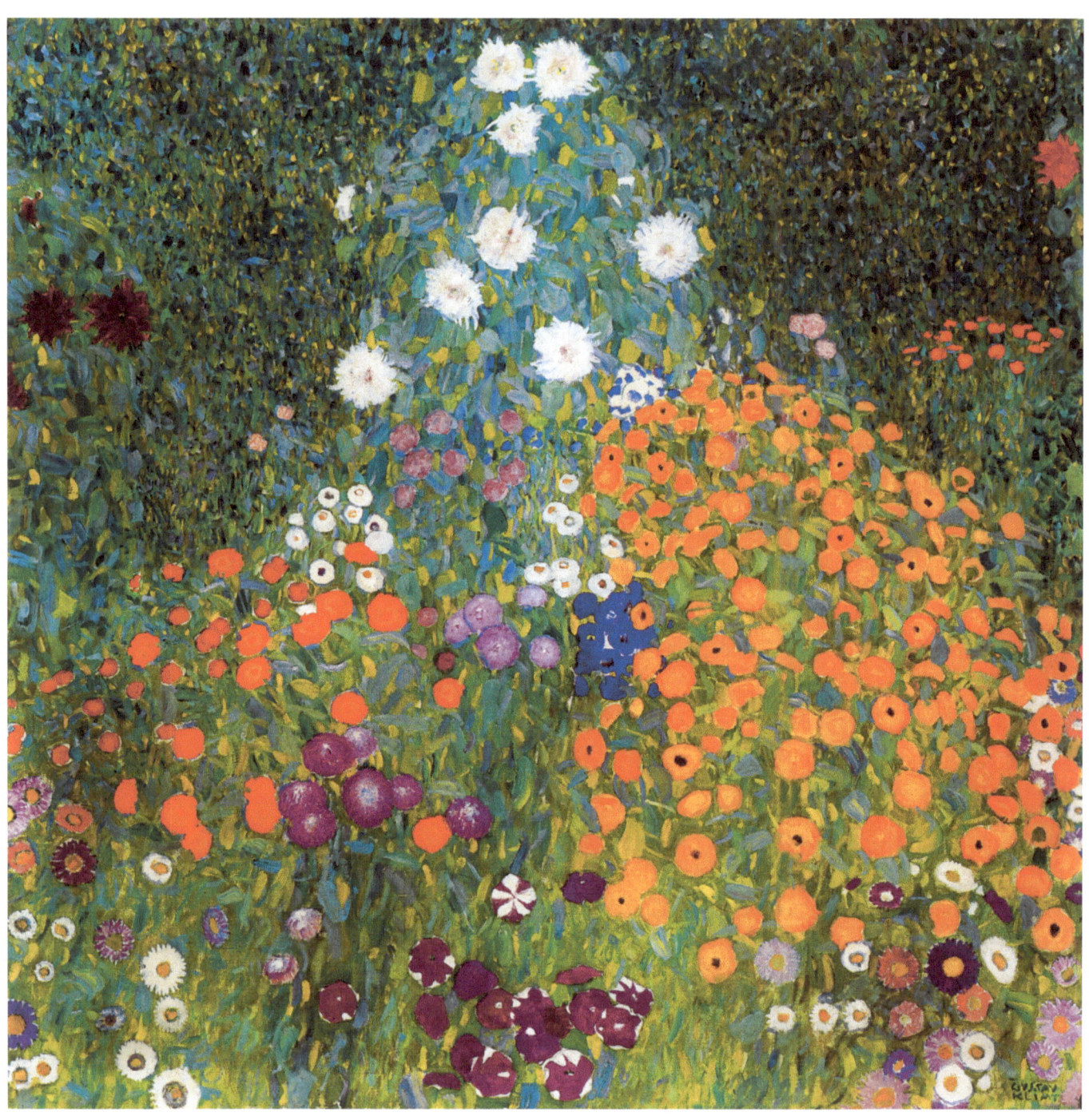

Chickens In Garden

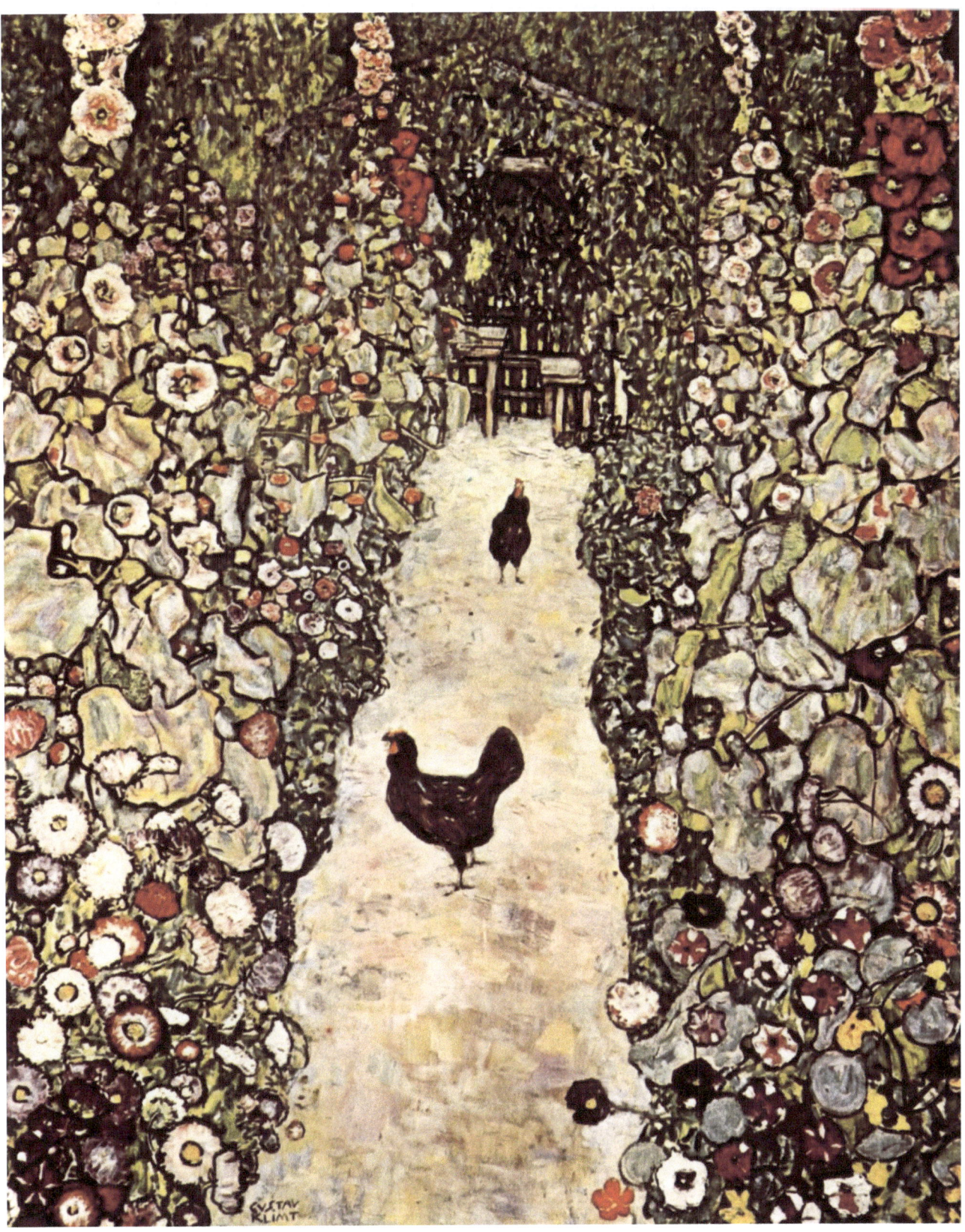

Houses at Unterach on the Attersee

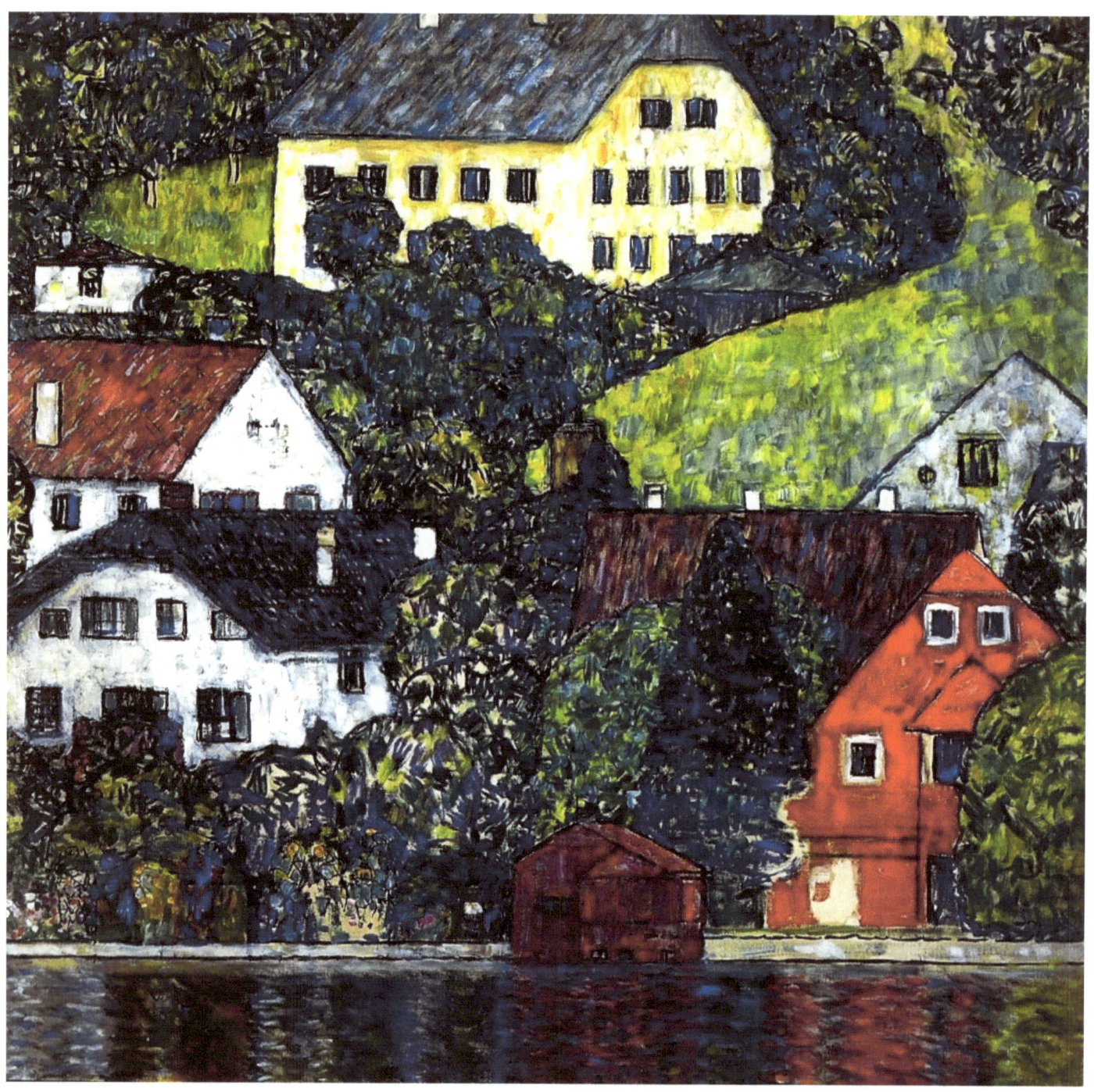

Mountain Slope at Unterach

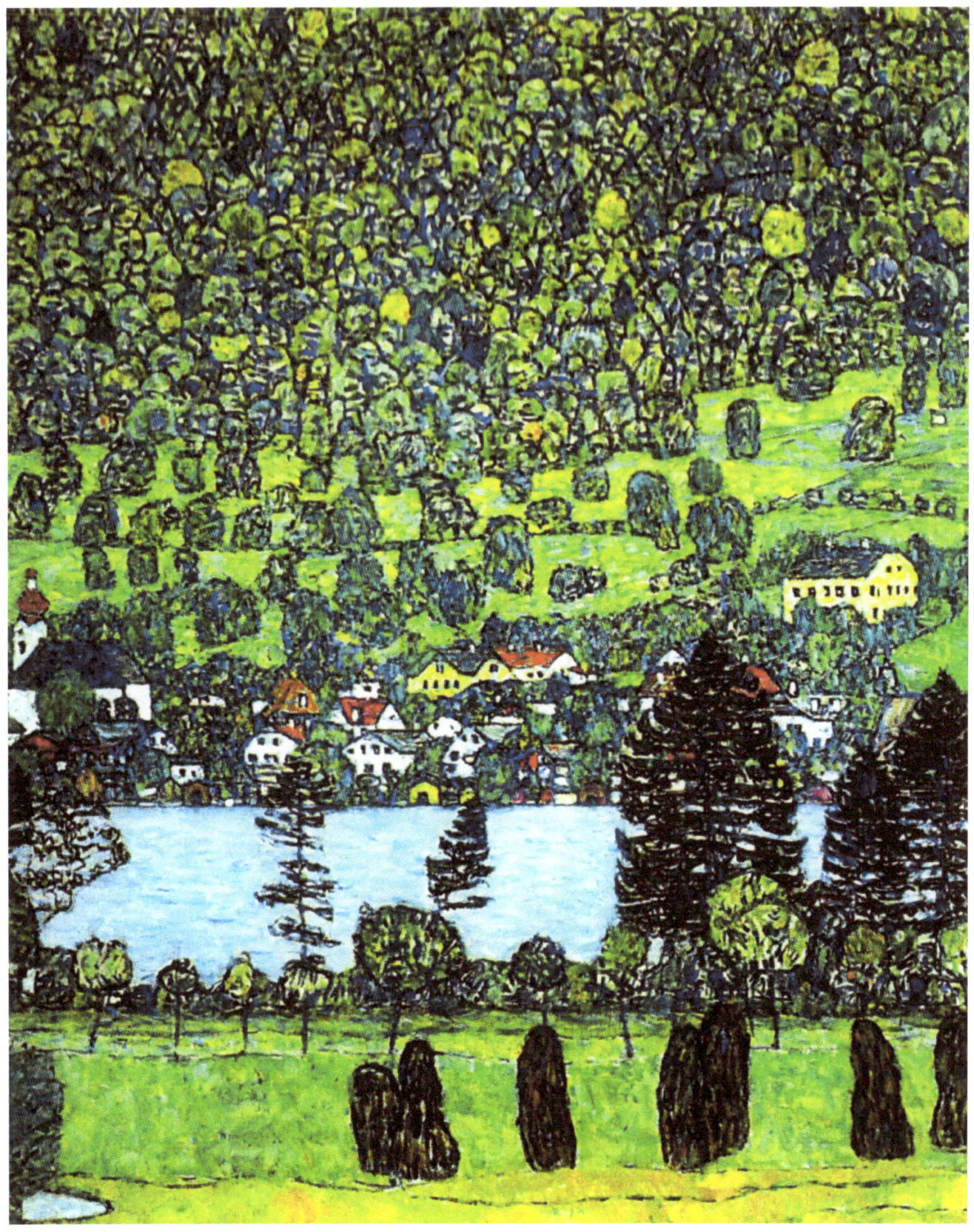

Large Poplar Tree And Coming Storm

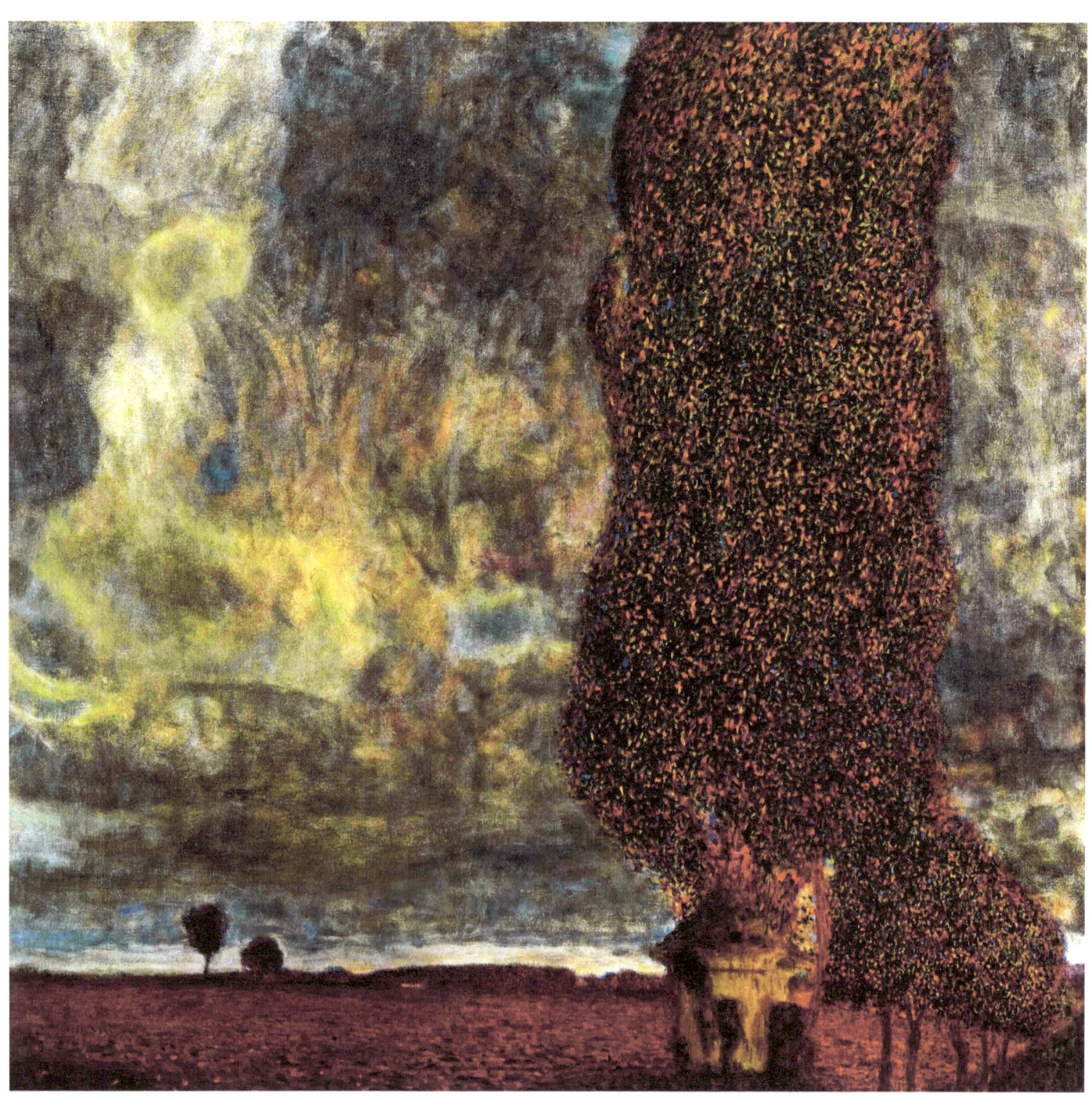

Orchard with Roses

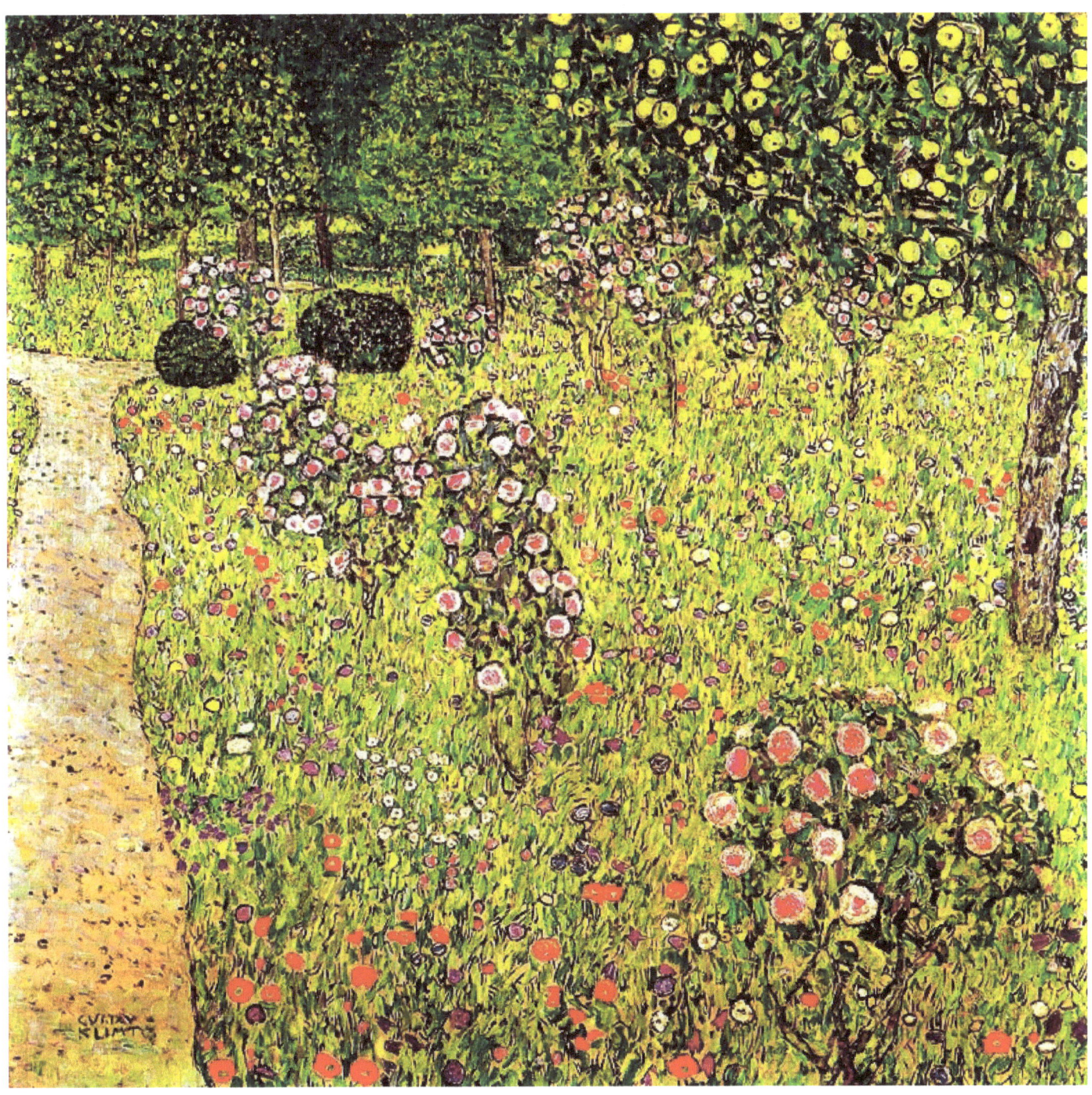

Attersea

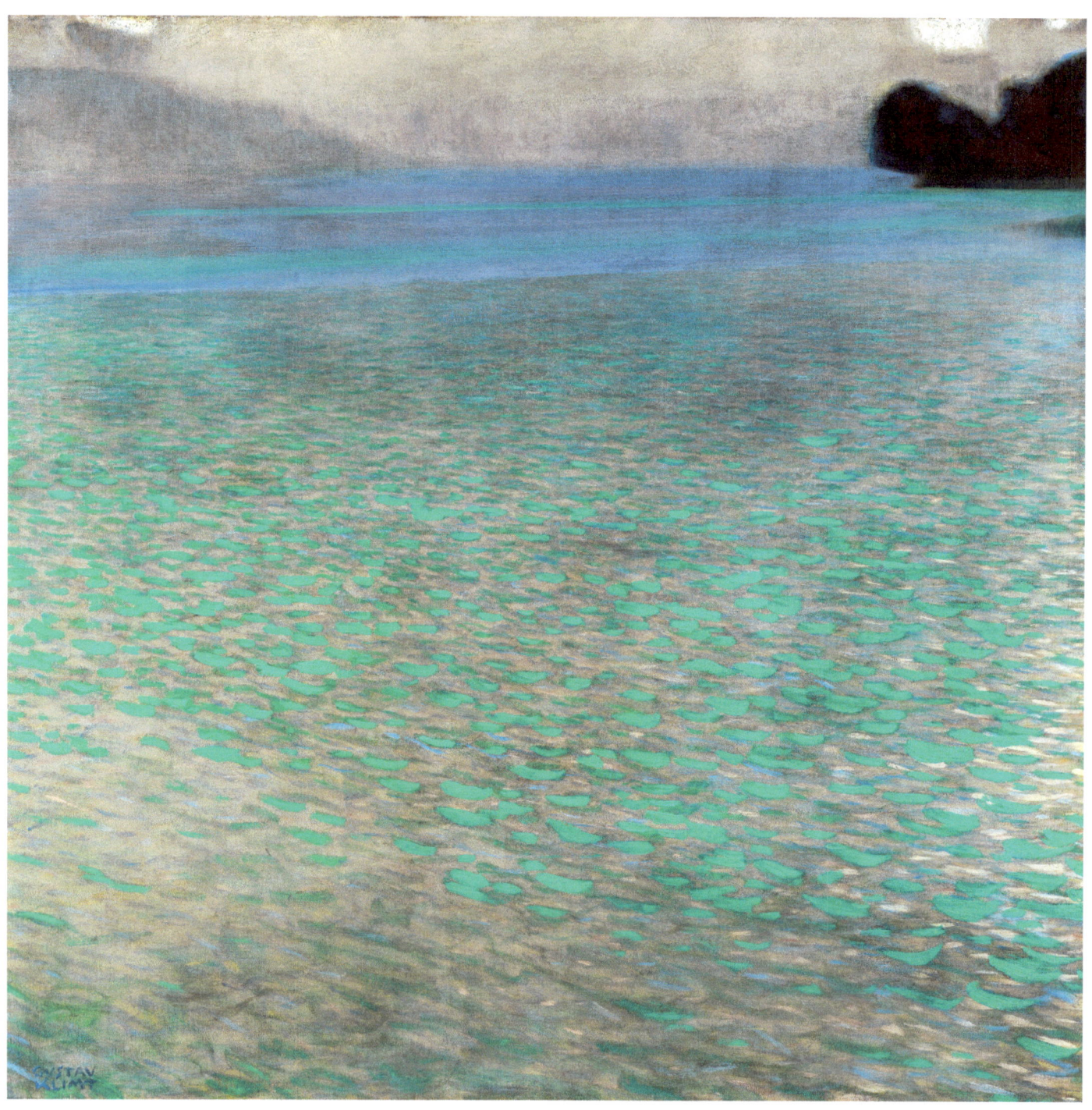

PEOPLE

Portrait of Mada Primavesi

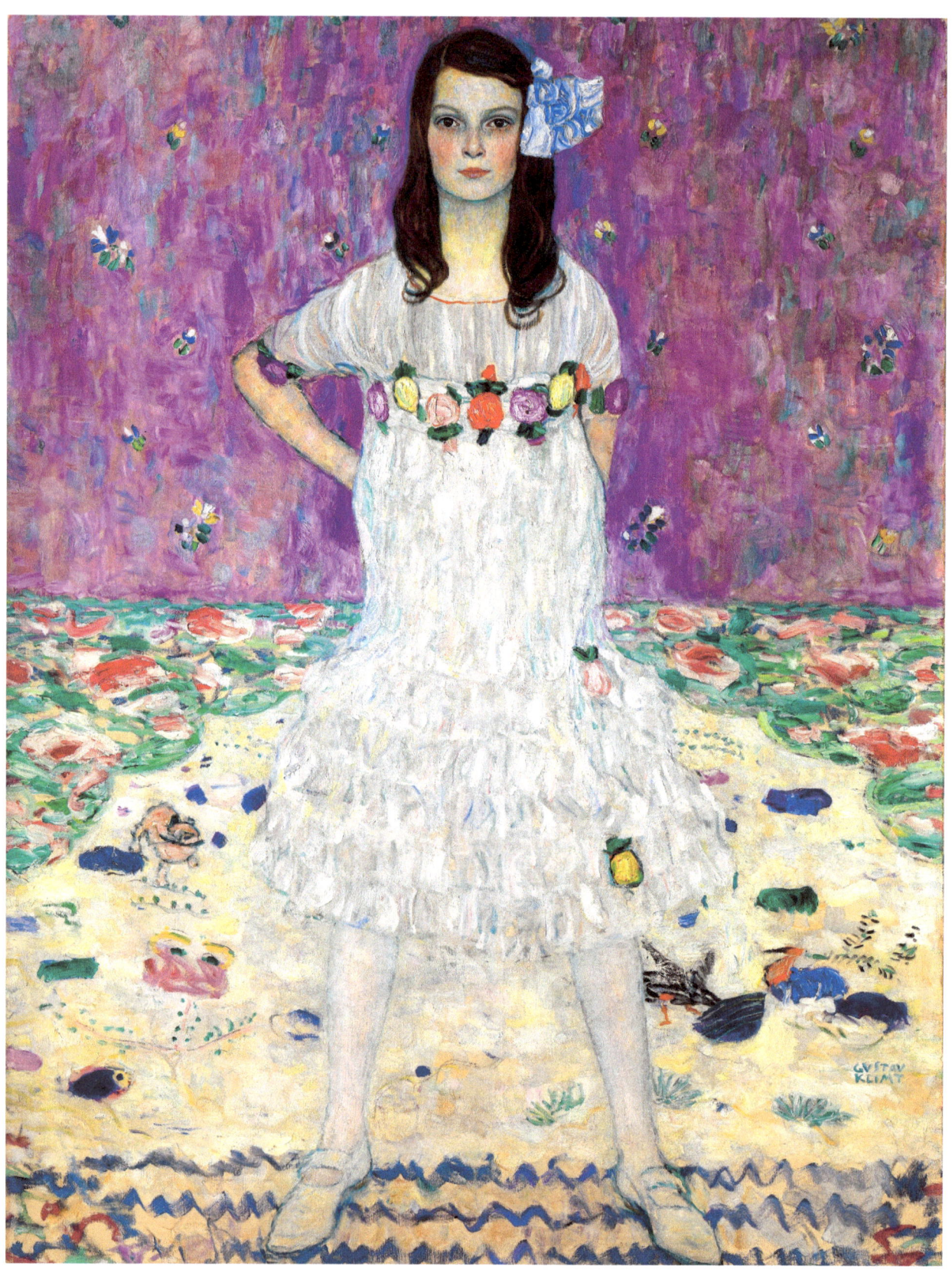

Blind Man

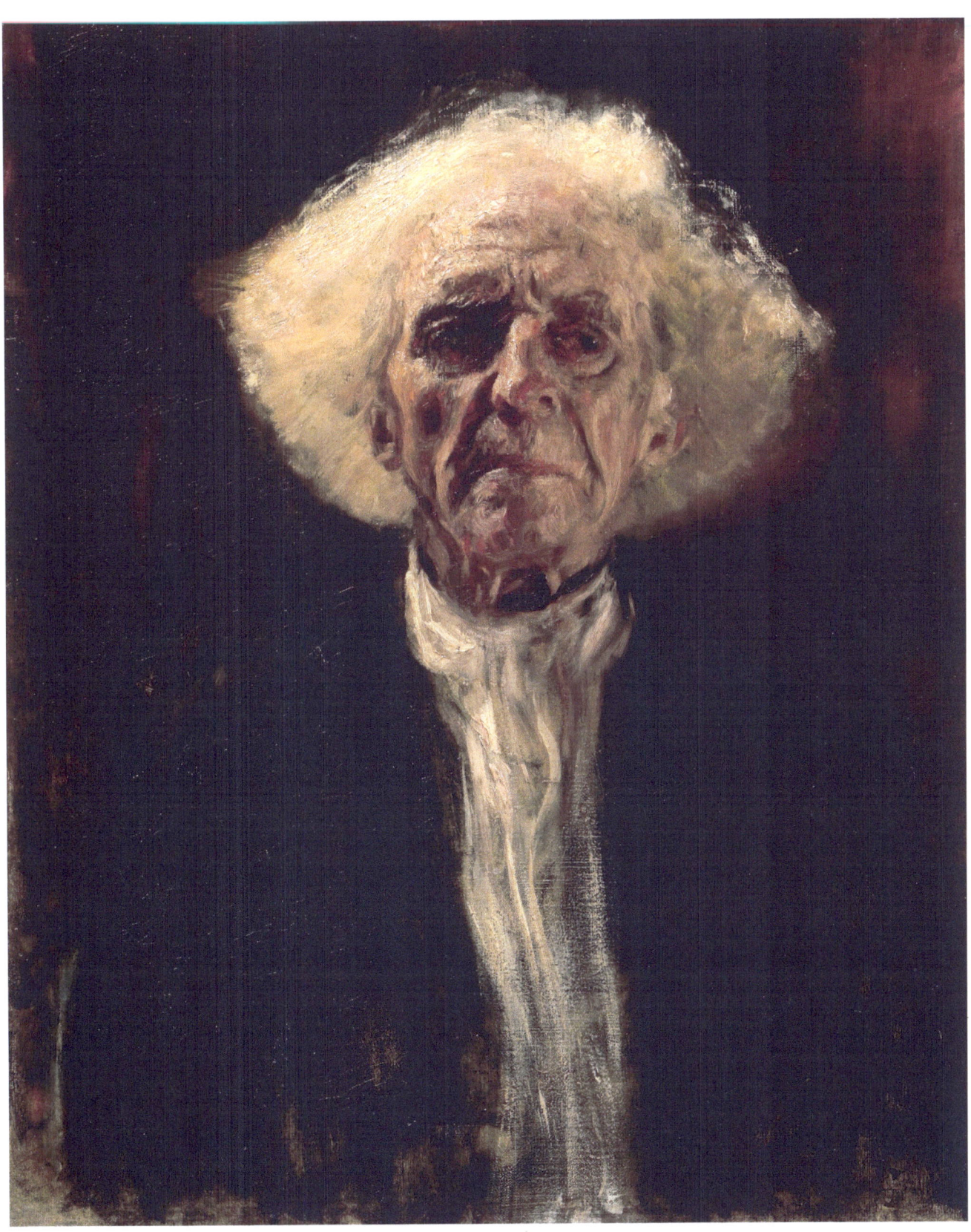

Lady With Fan

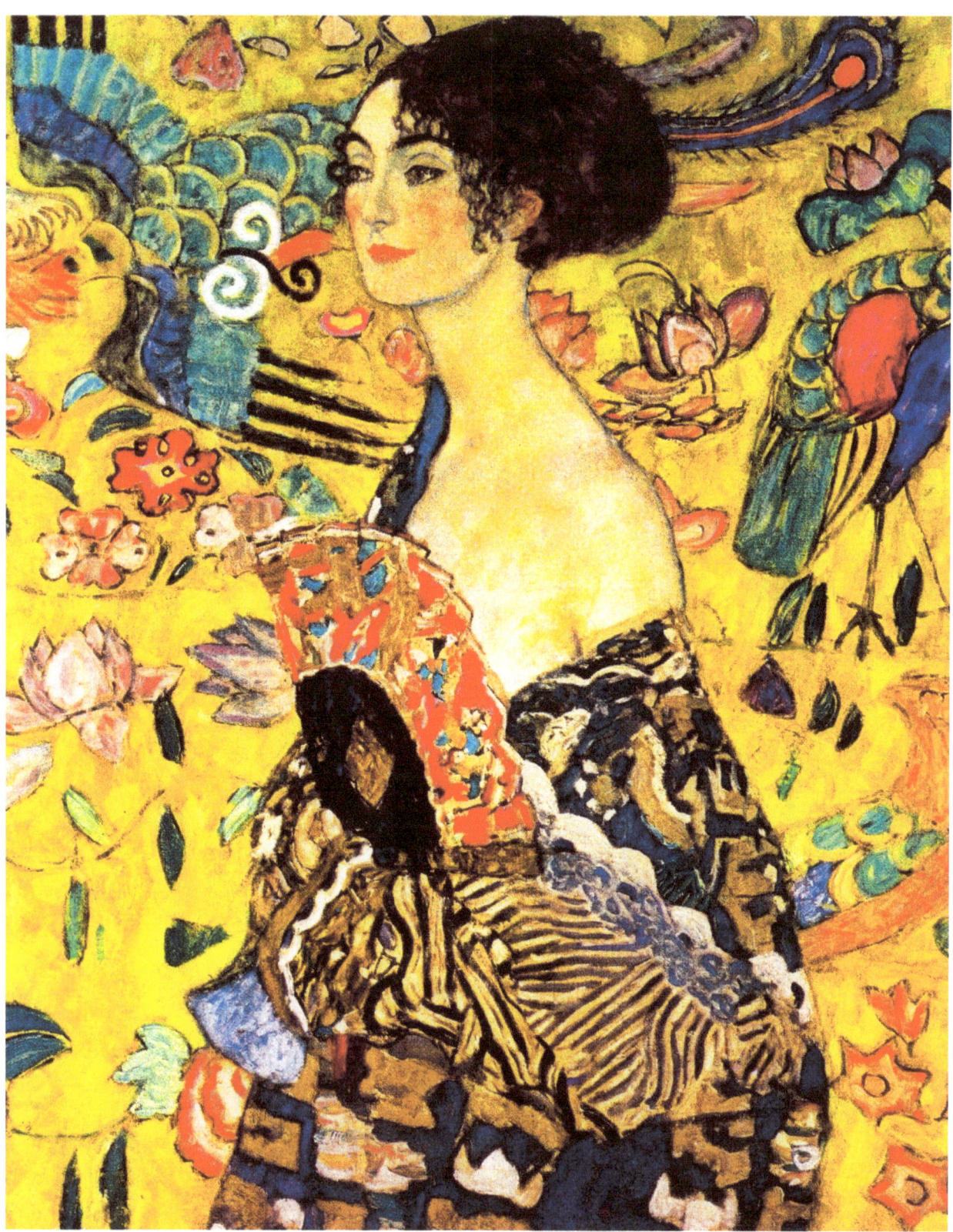

The Kiss

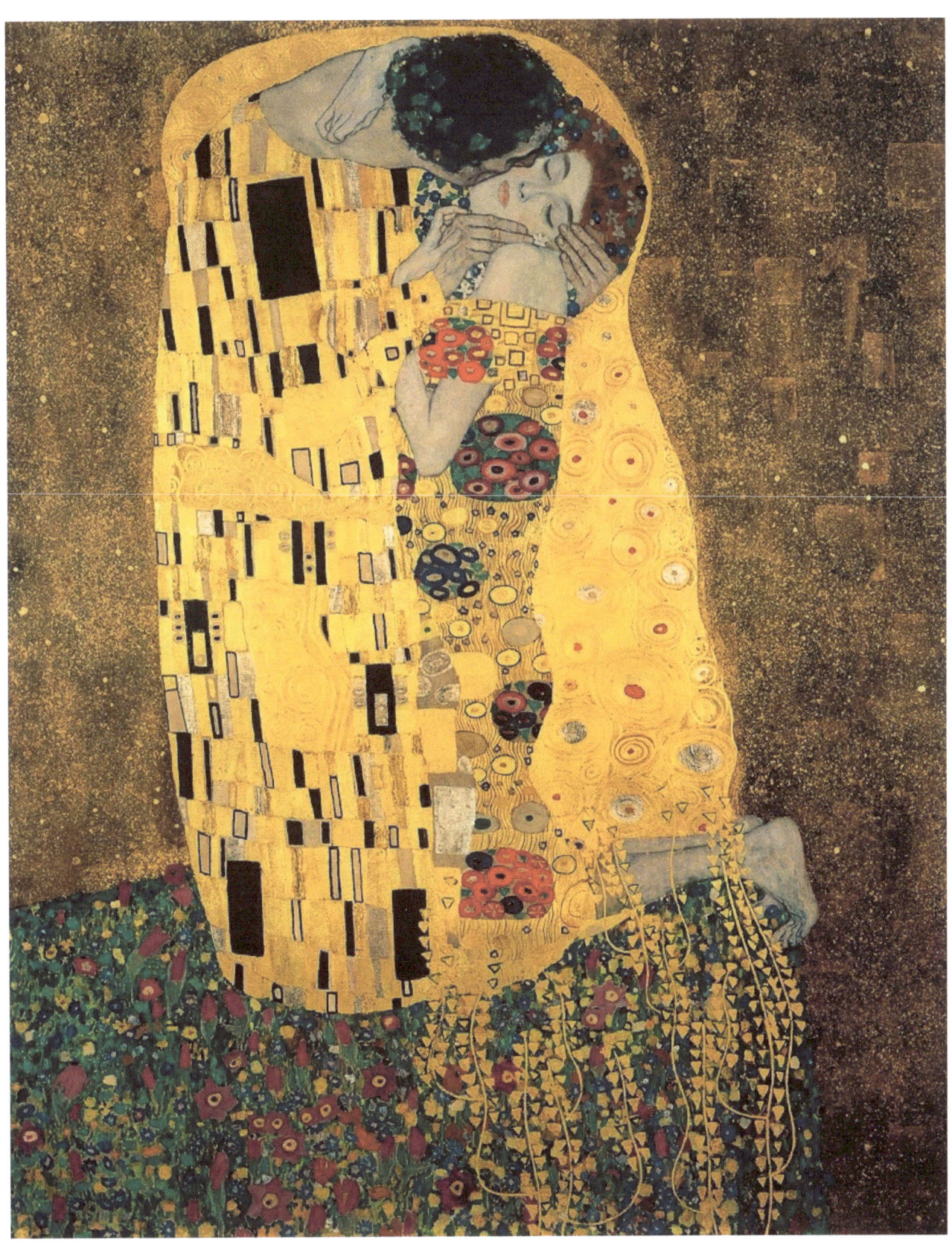

Portrait of Adele Bloch Bauer

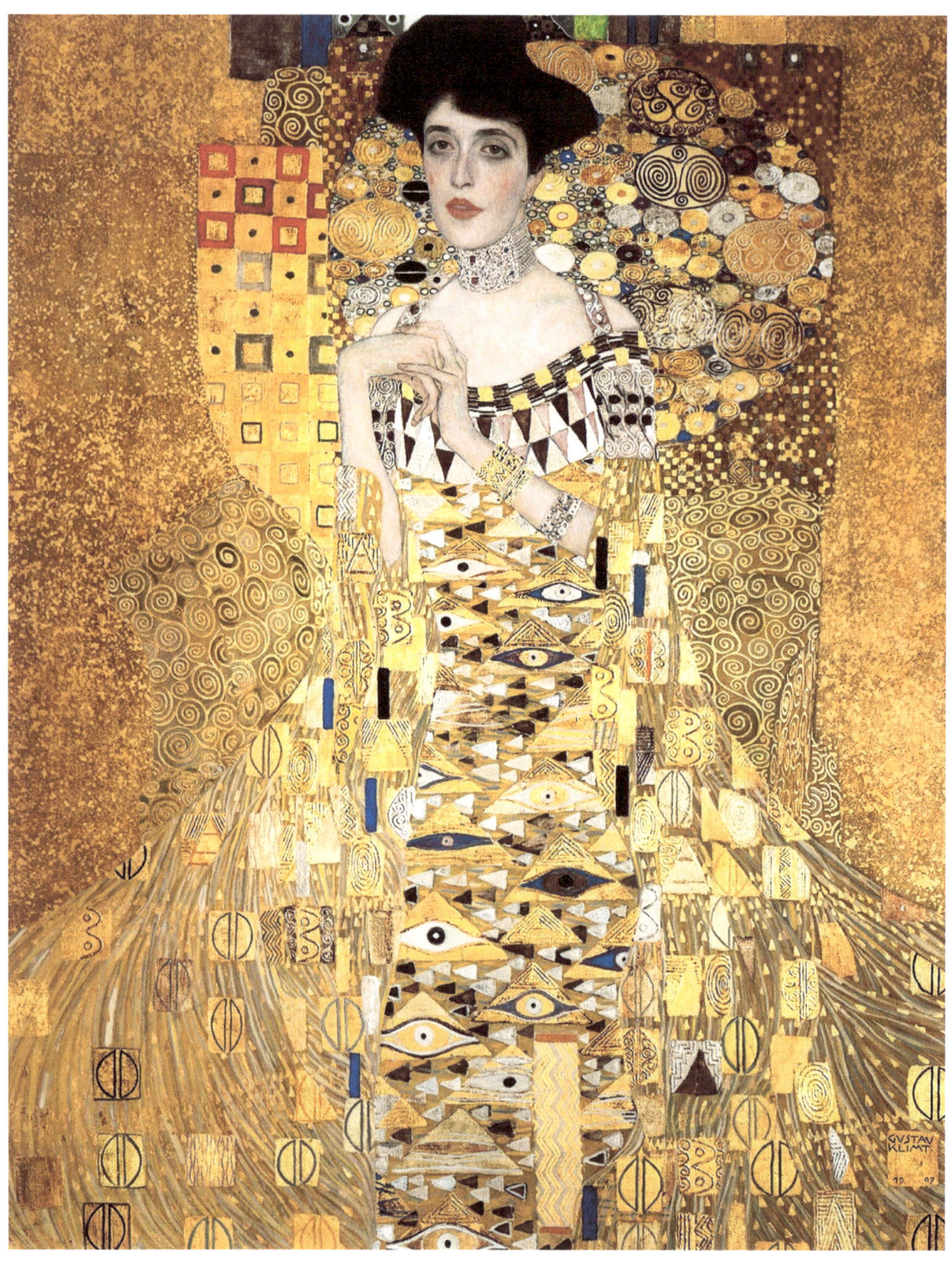

Portrait of Man With Beard

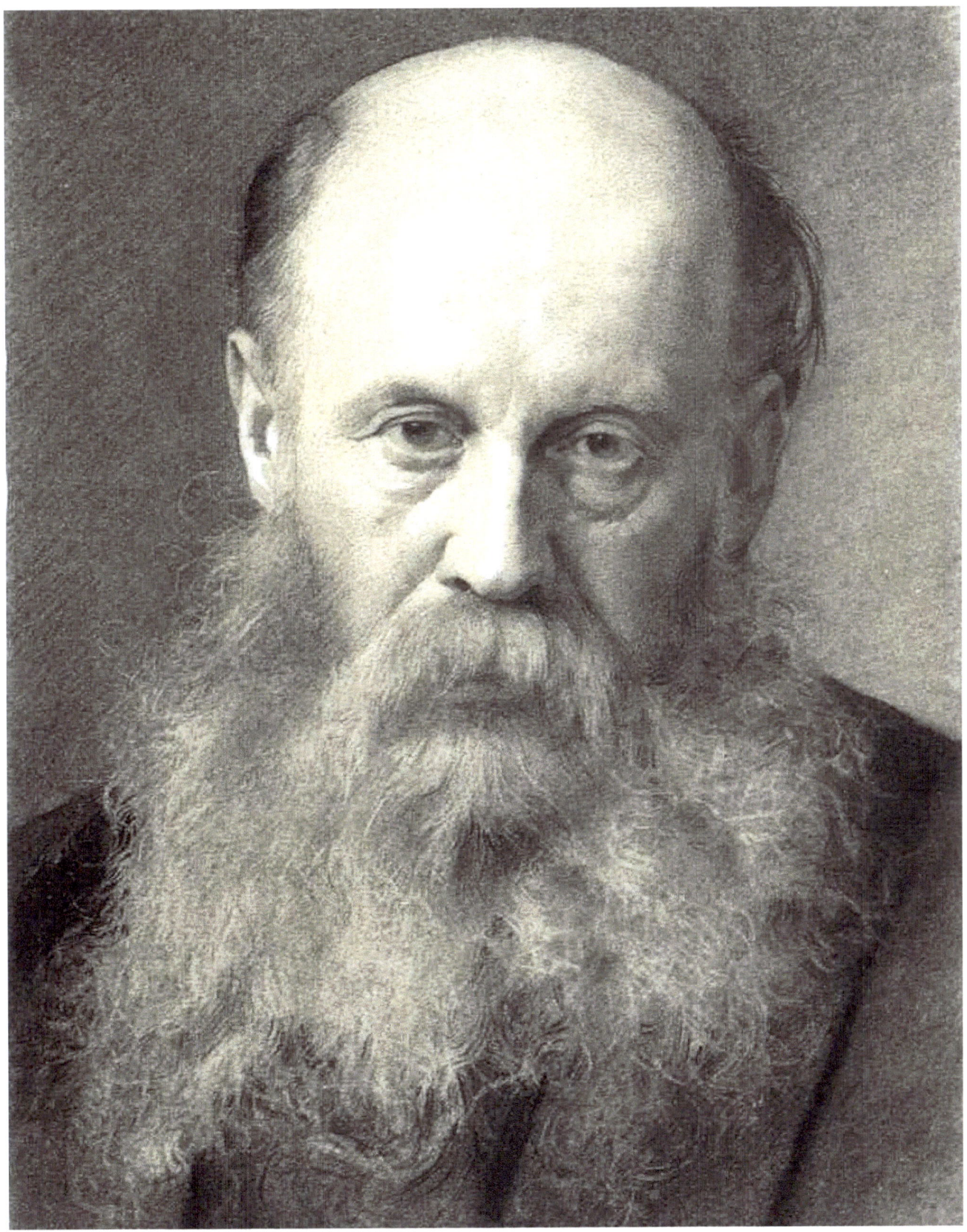

Portrait of Frieda Reidel

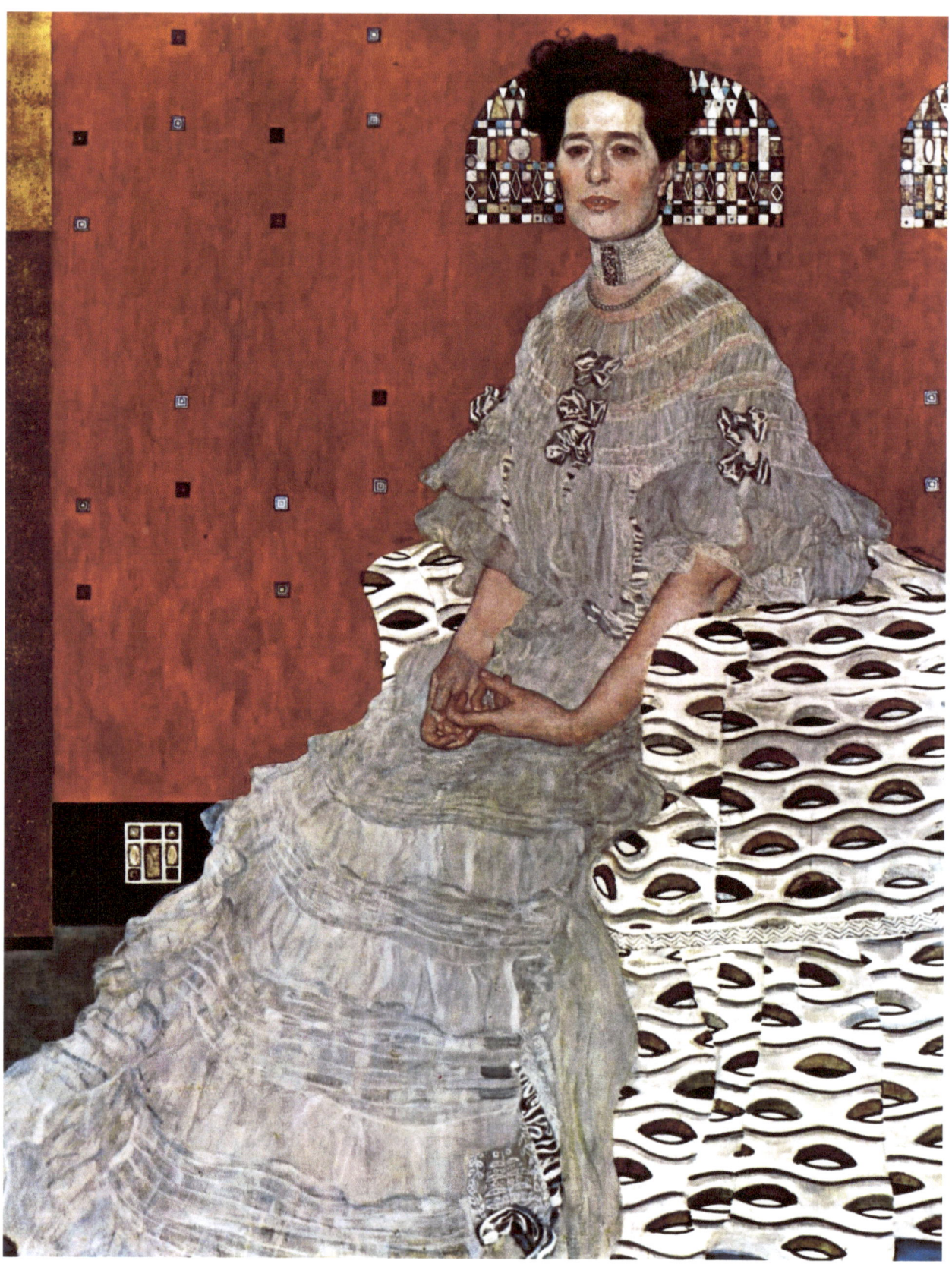

Portrait of Young Woman Reclining

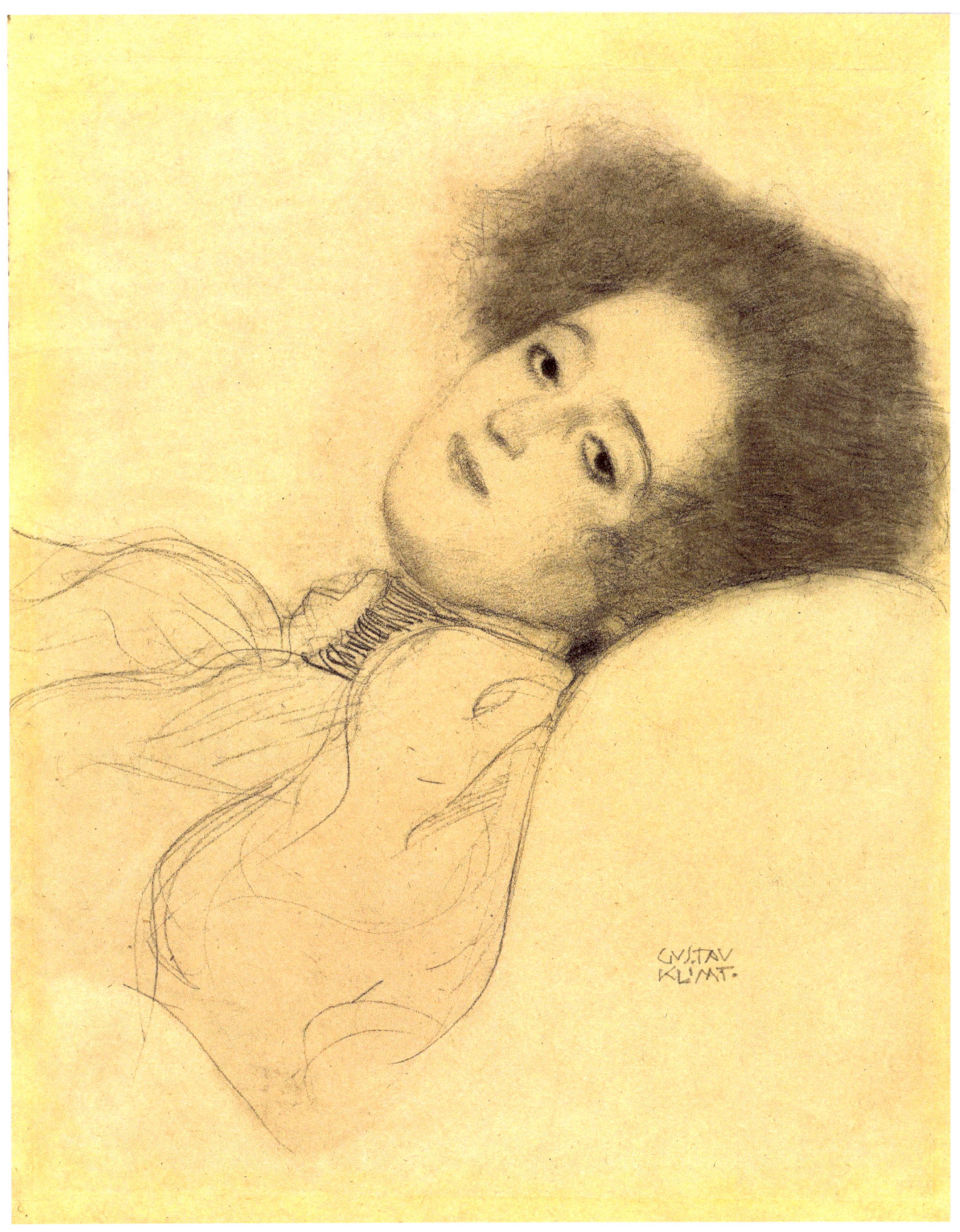

Portrait of an Old Man Wearing an Ivy Wreath

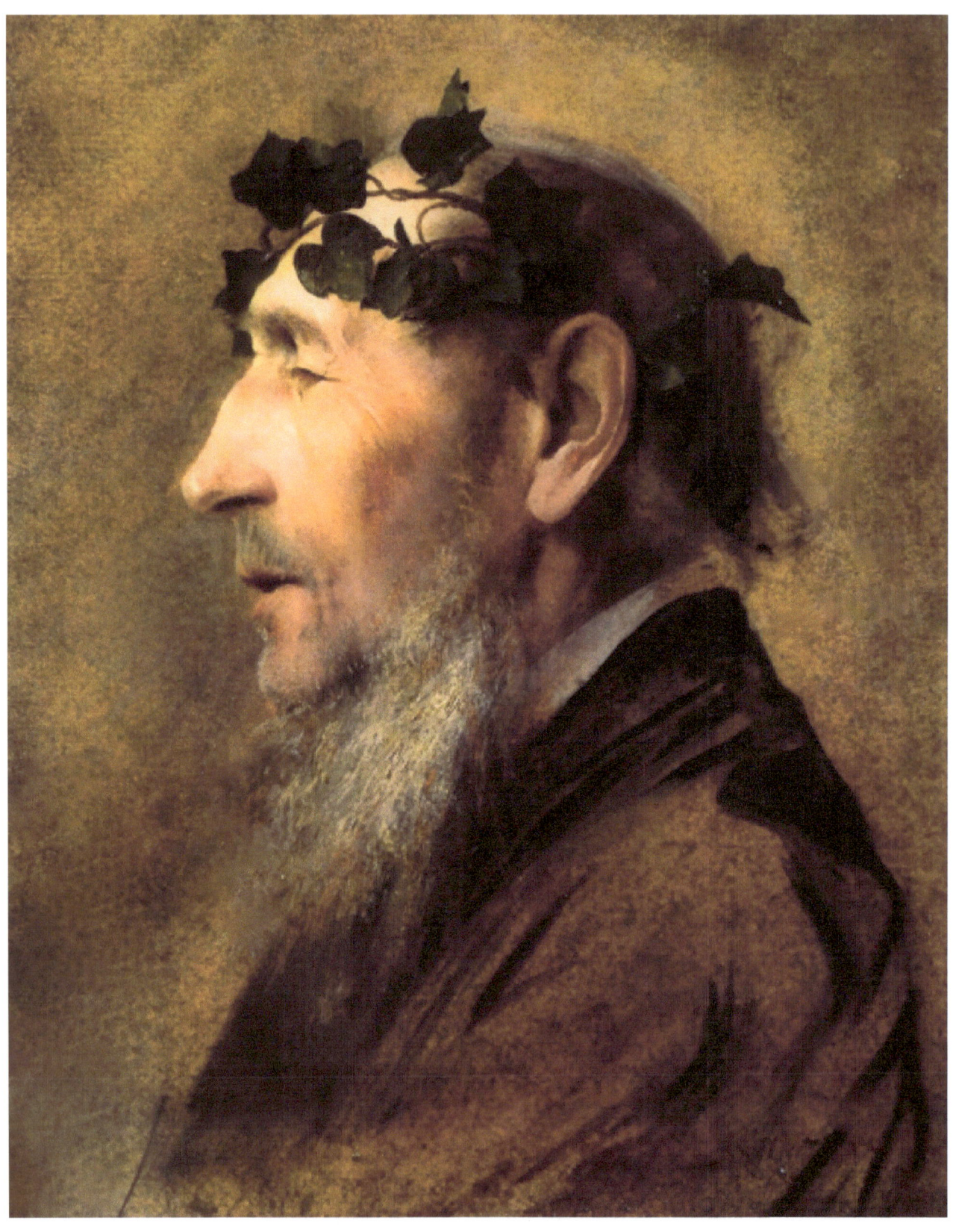

Portrait of a Lady

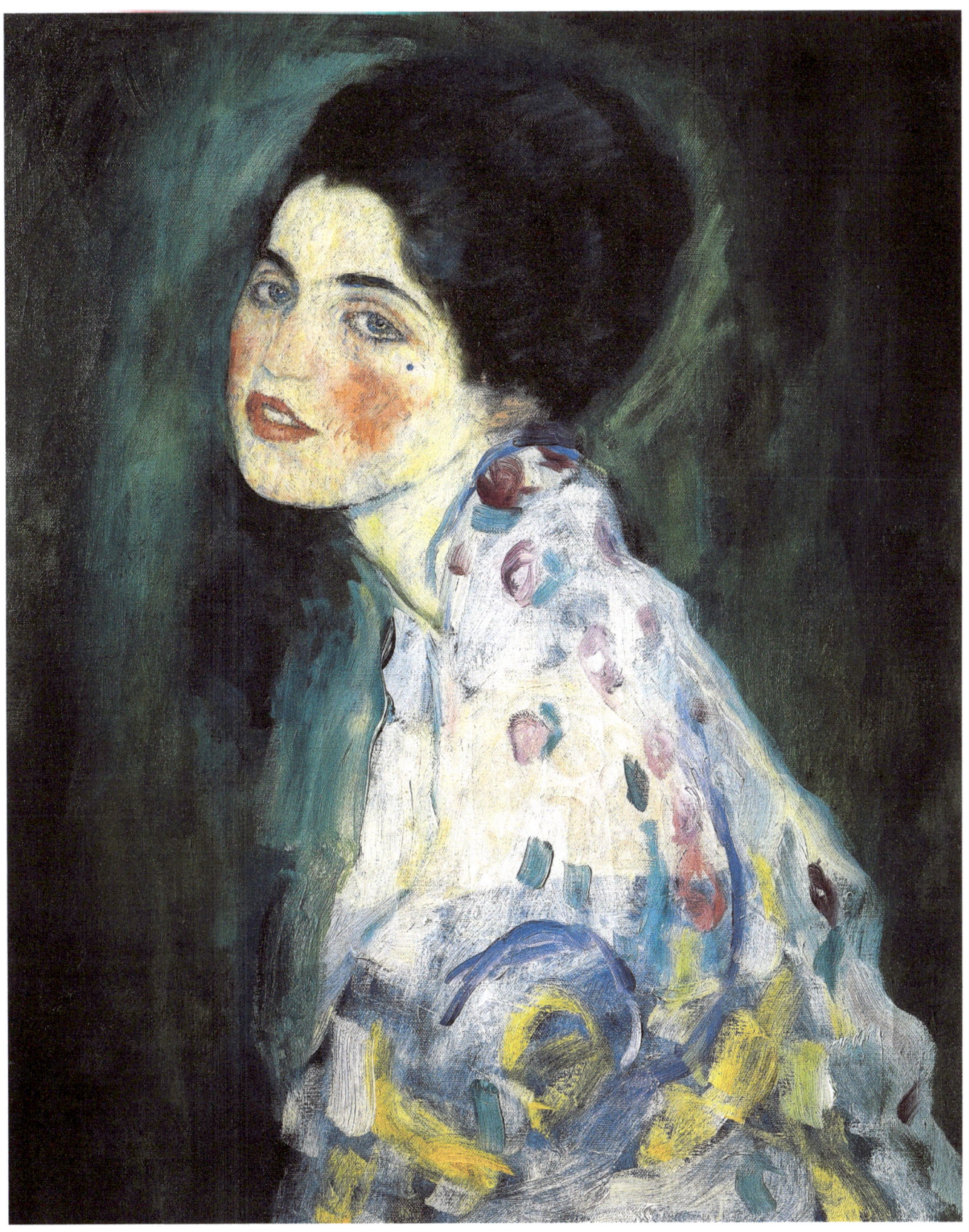

Woman in White Dress

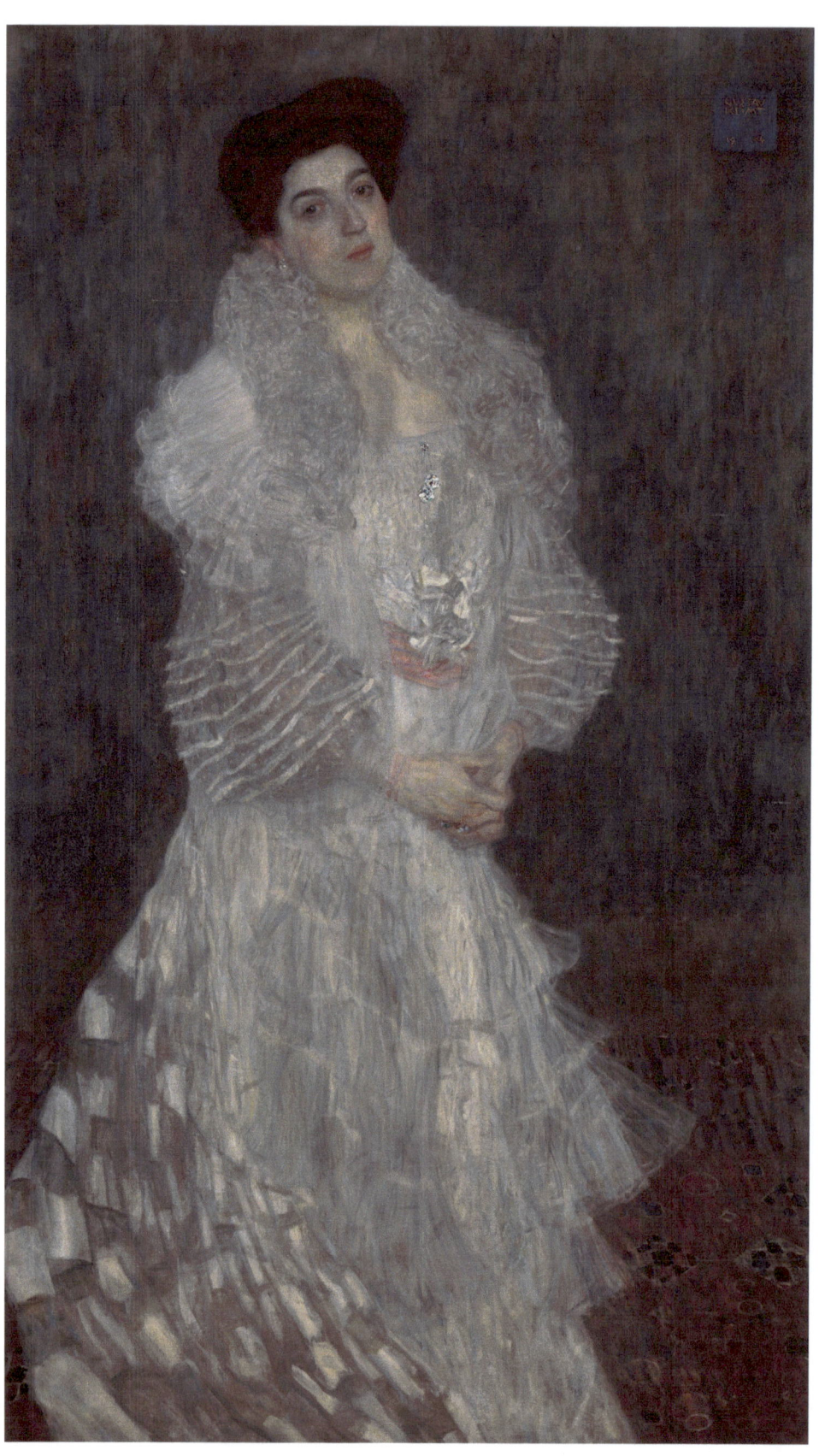

Portrait of the Artist's Dead Son

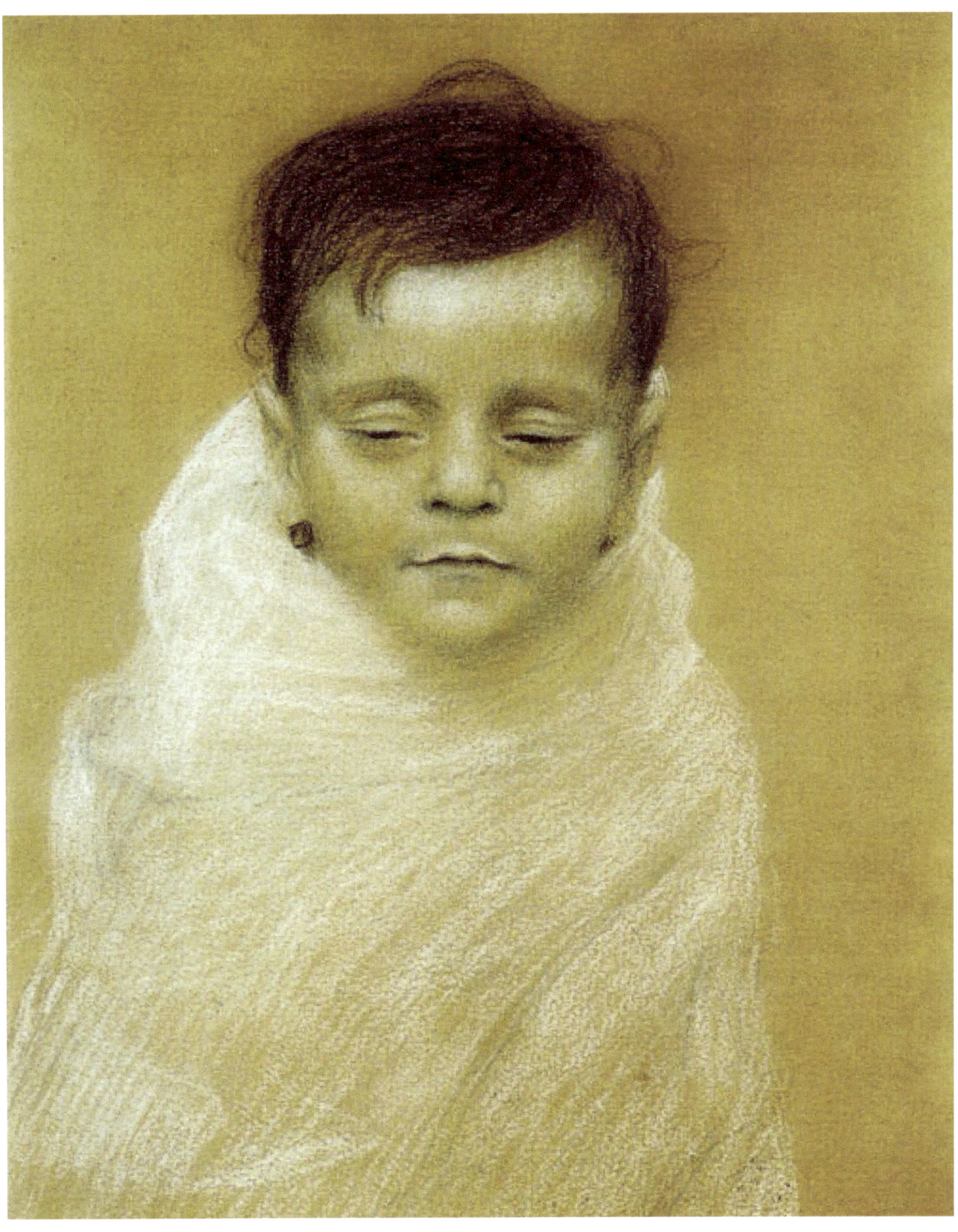

Baby Cradle

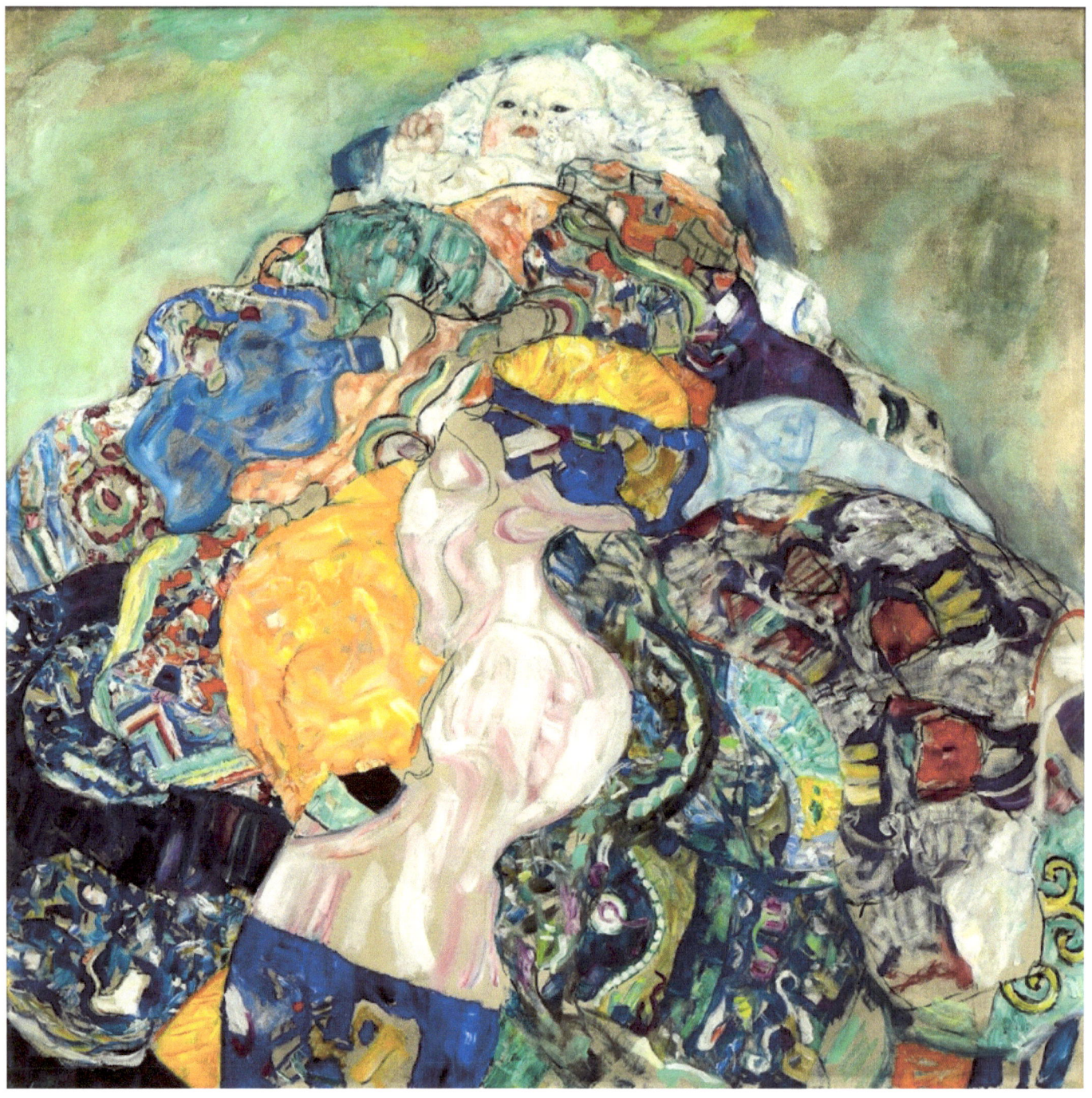

Portrait of a Woman in an Armchair

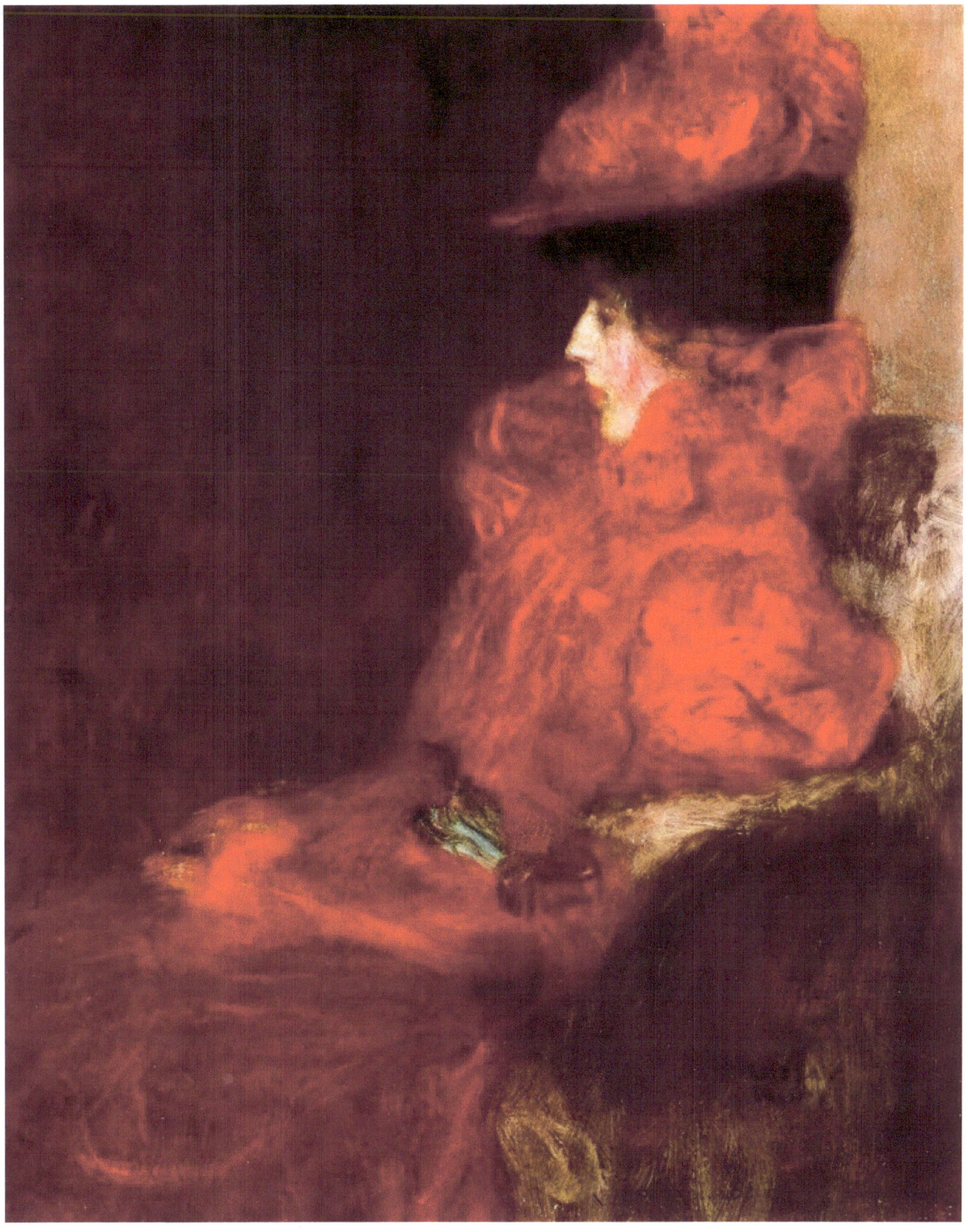

NUDES

Eve and Adam

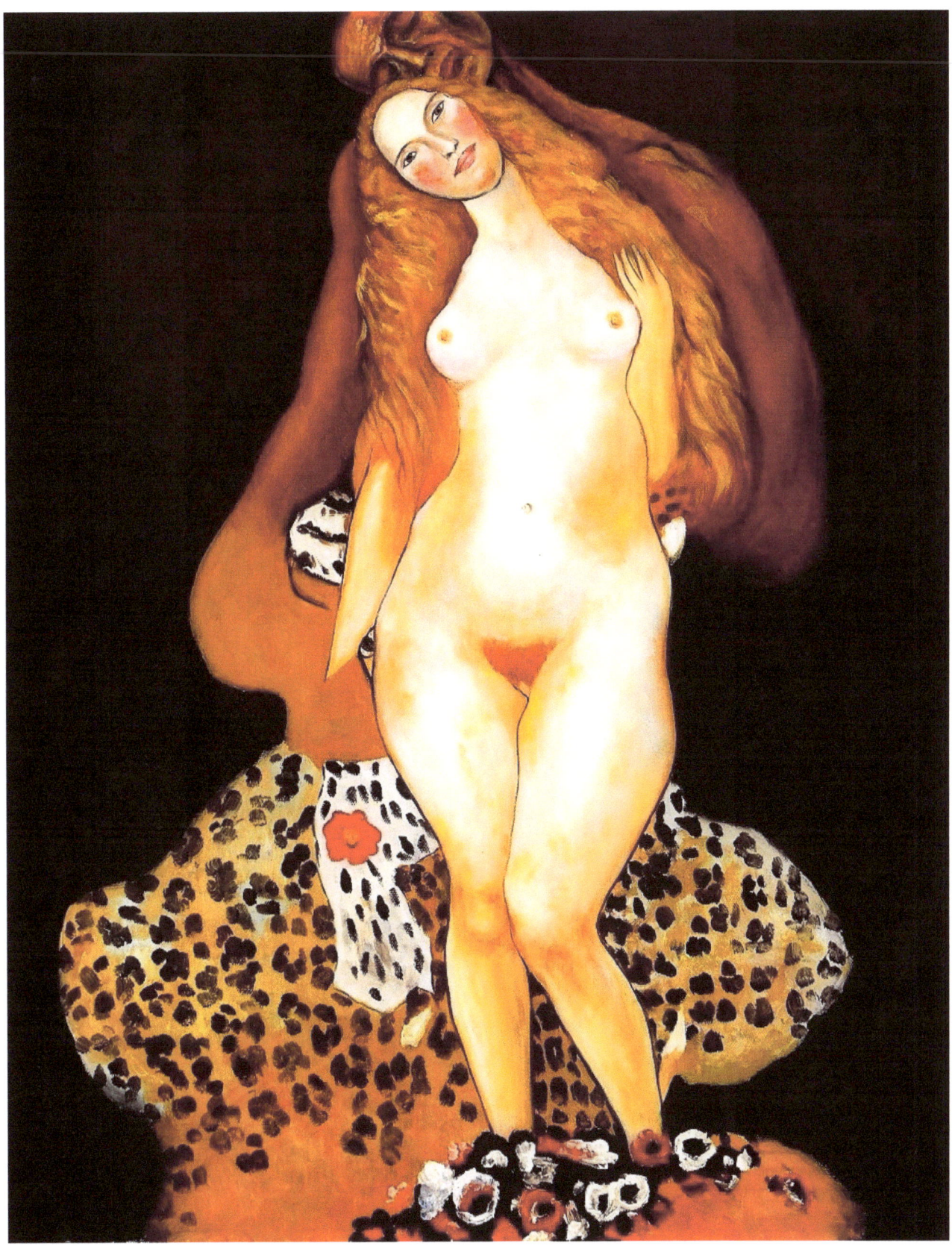

Salomé

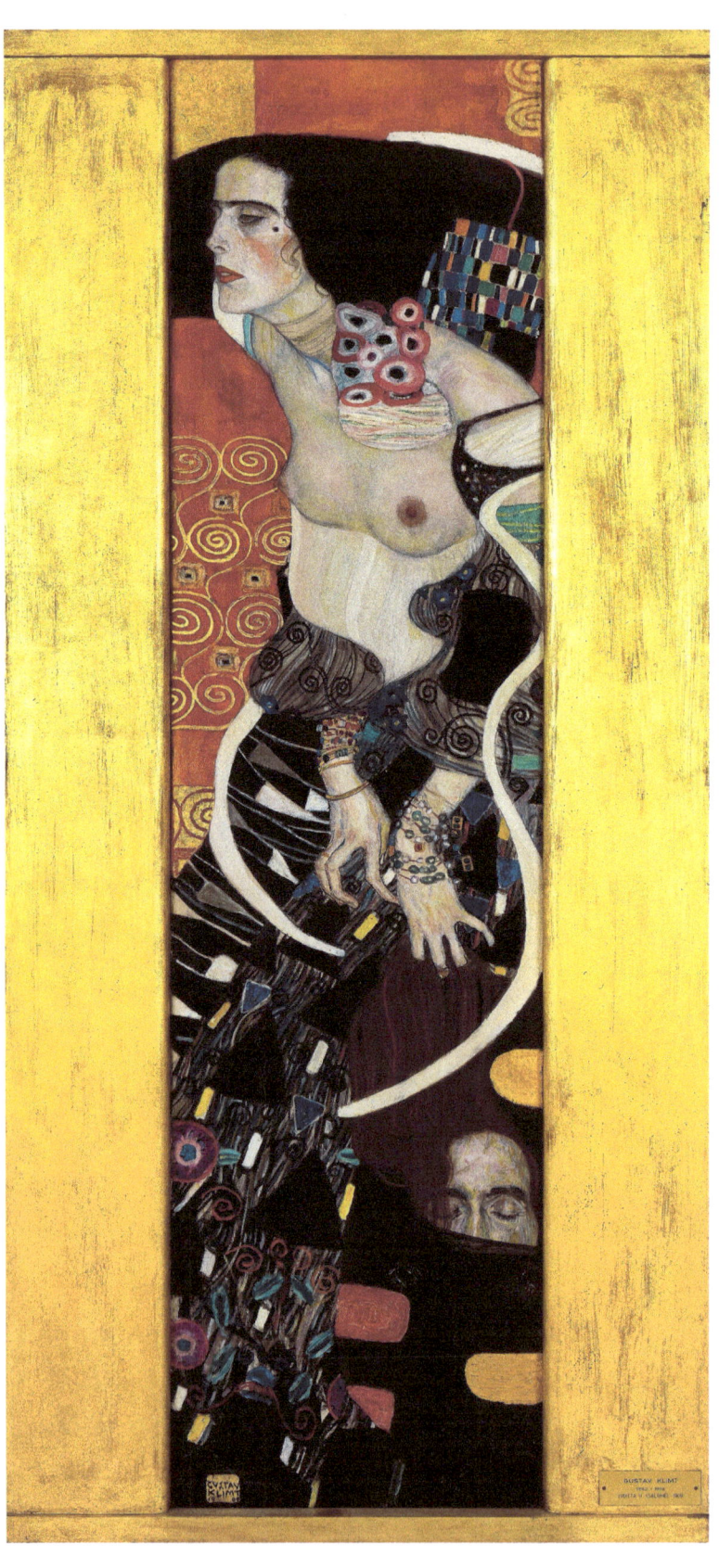

The Maiden

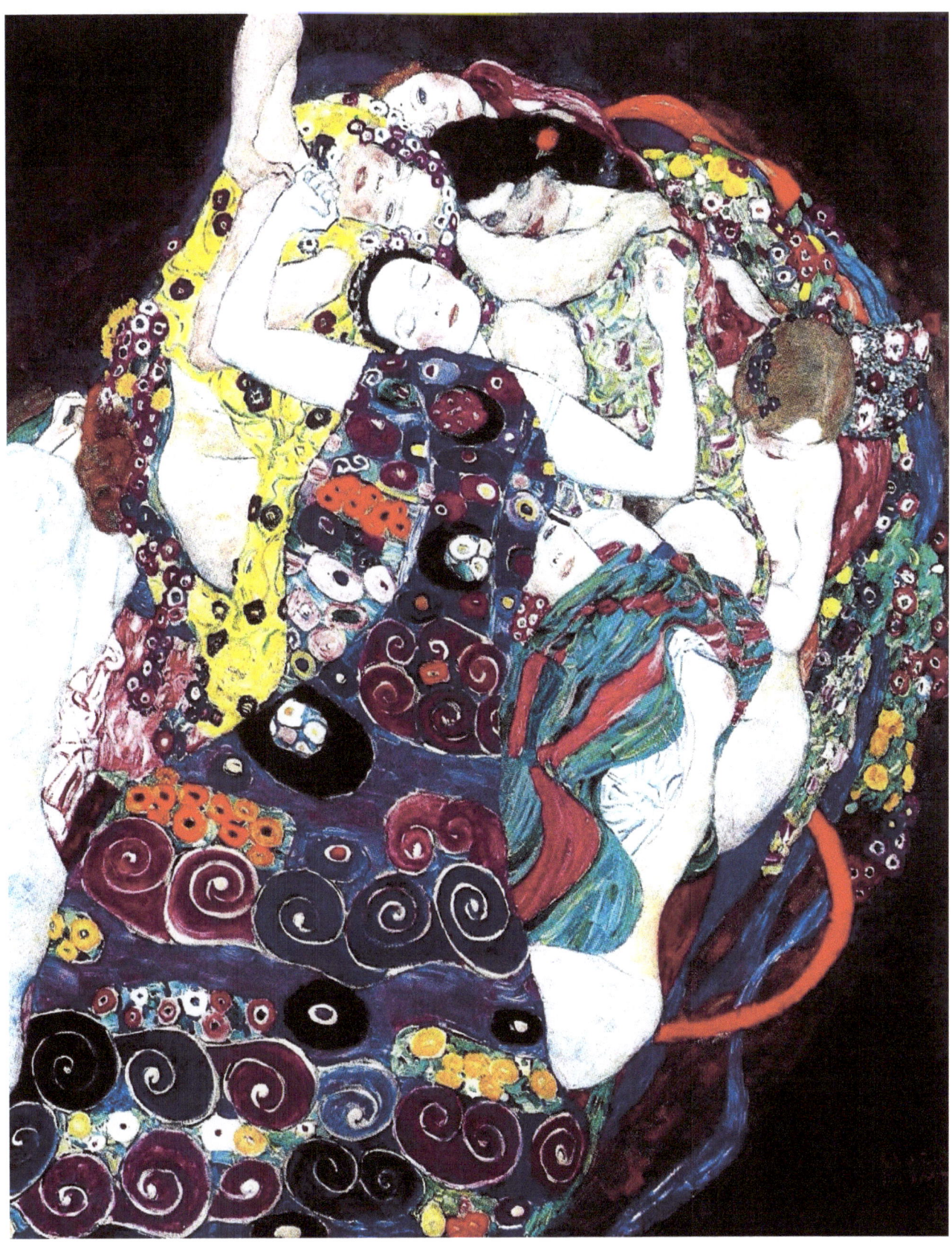

Allegory of a Statue

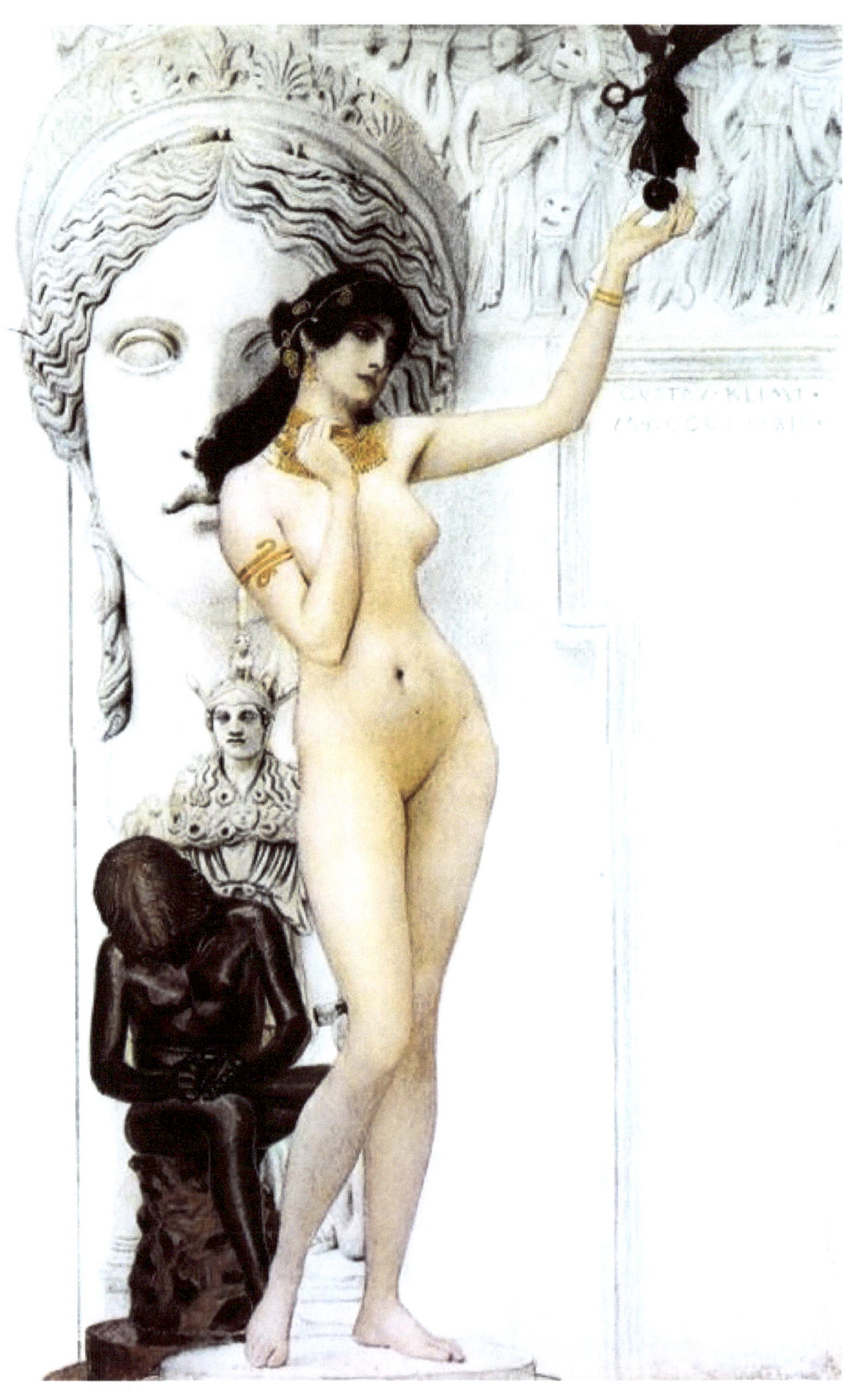

Mother and Child

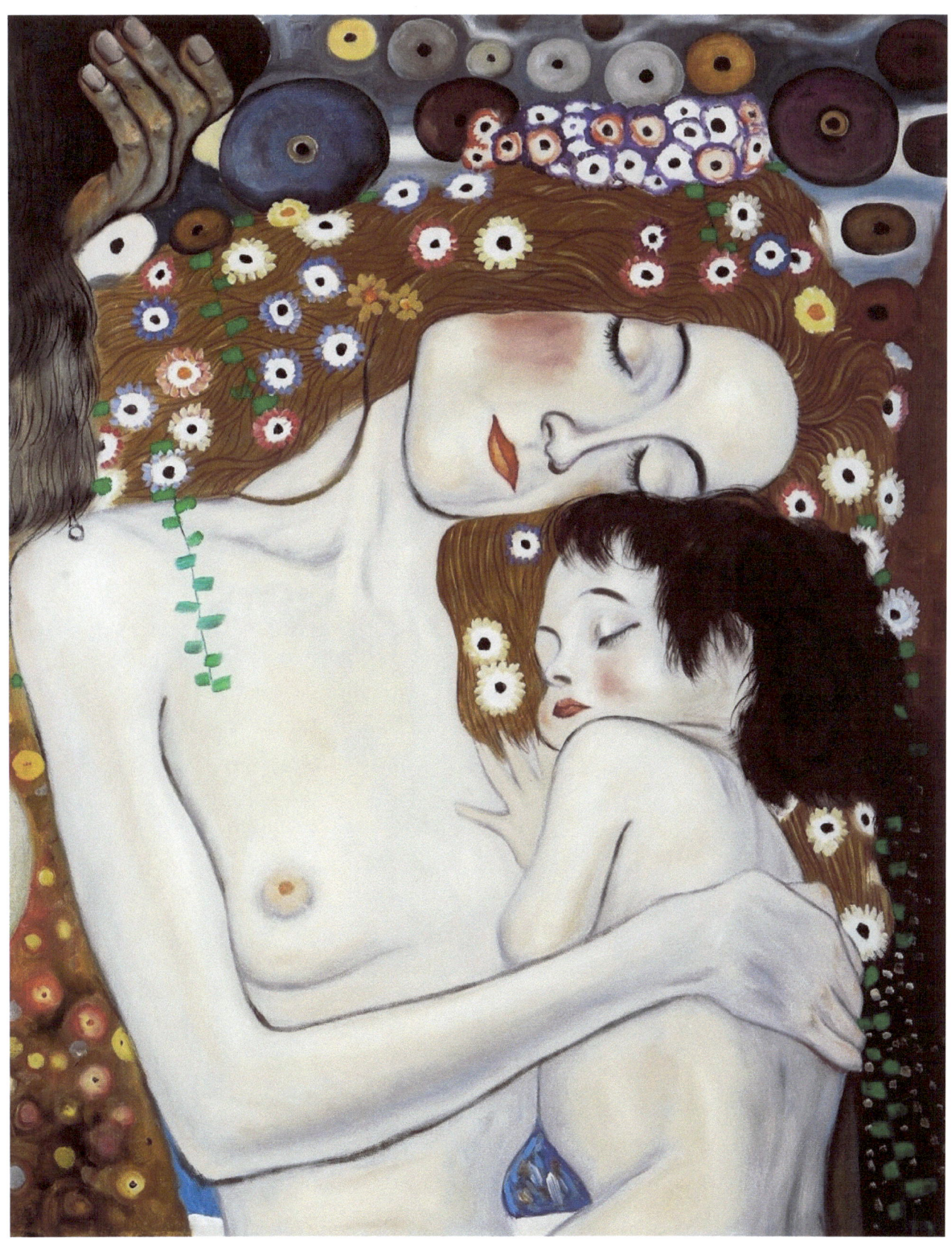

Two Studies of a Seated Nude with Long Hair

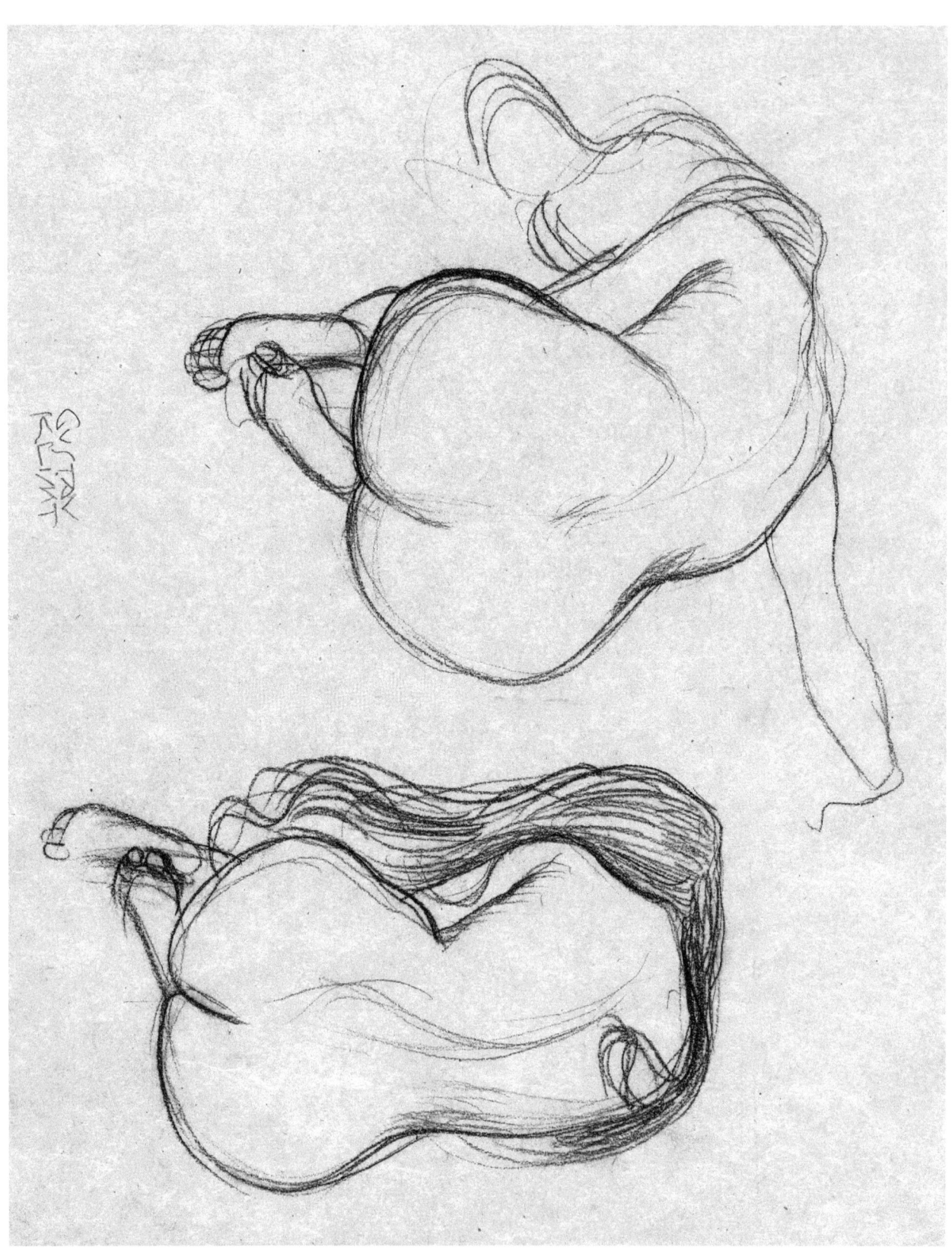

Hope II

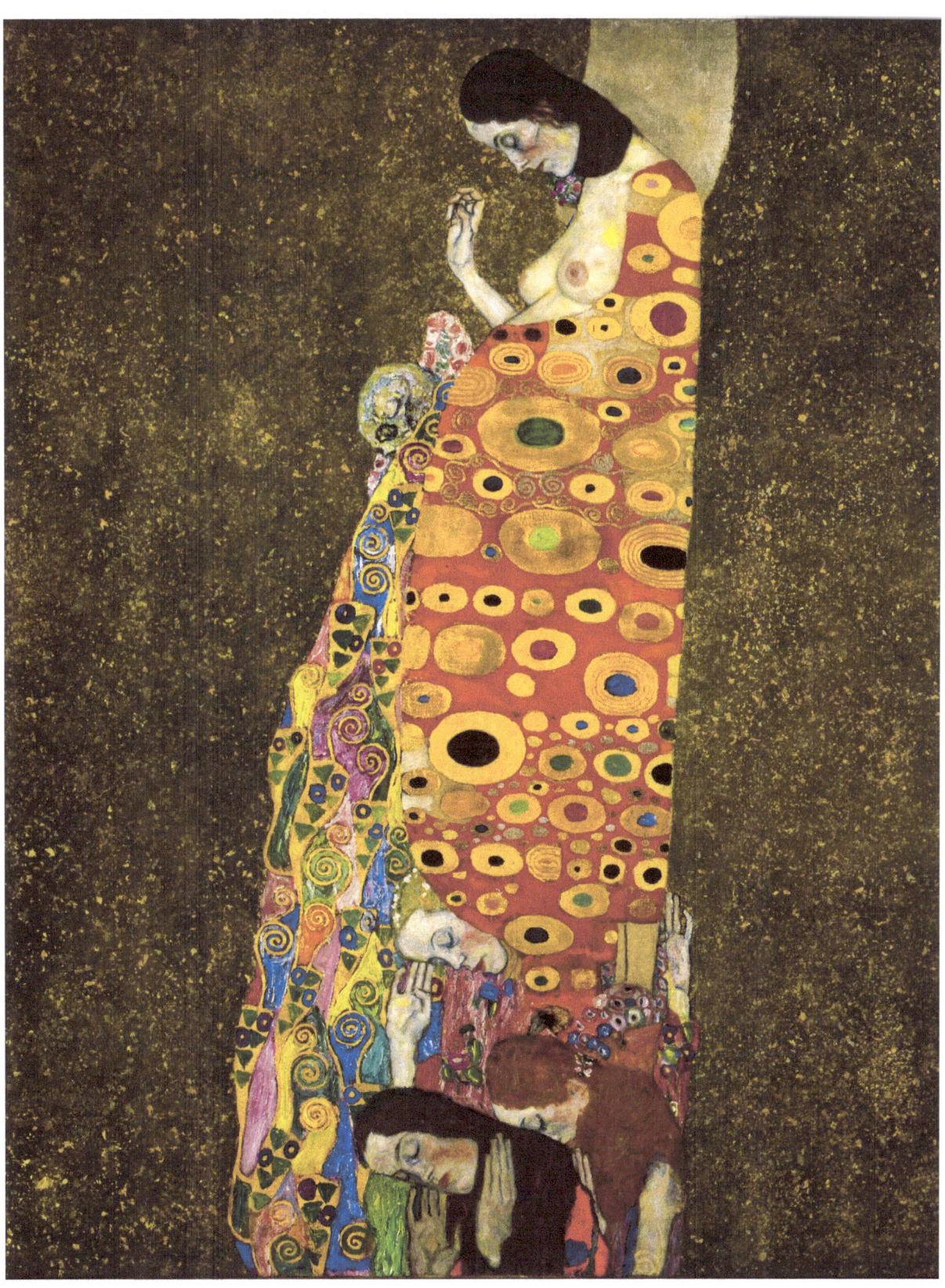

Two Friends

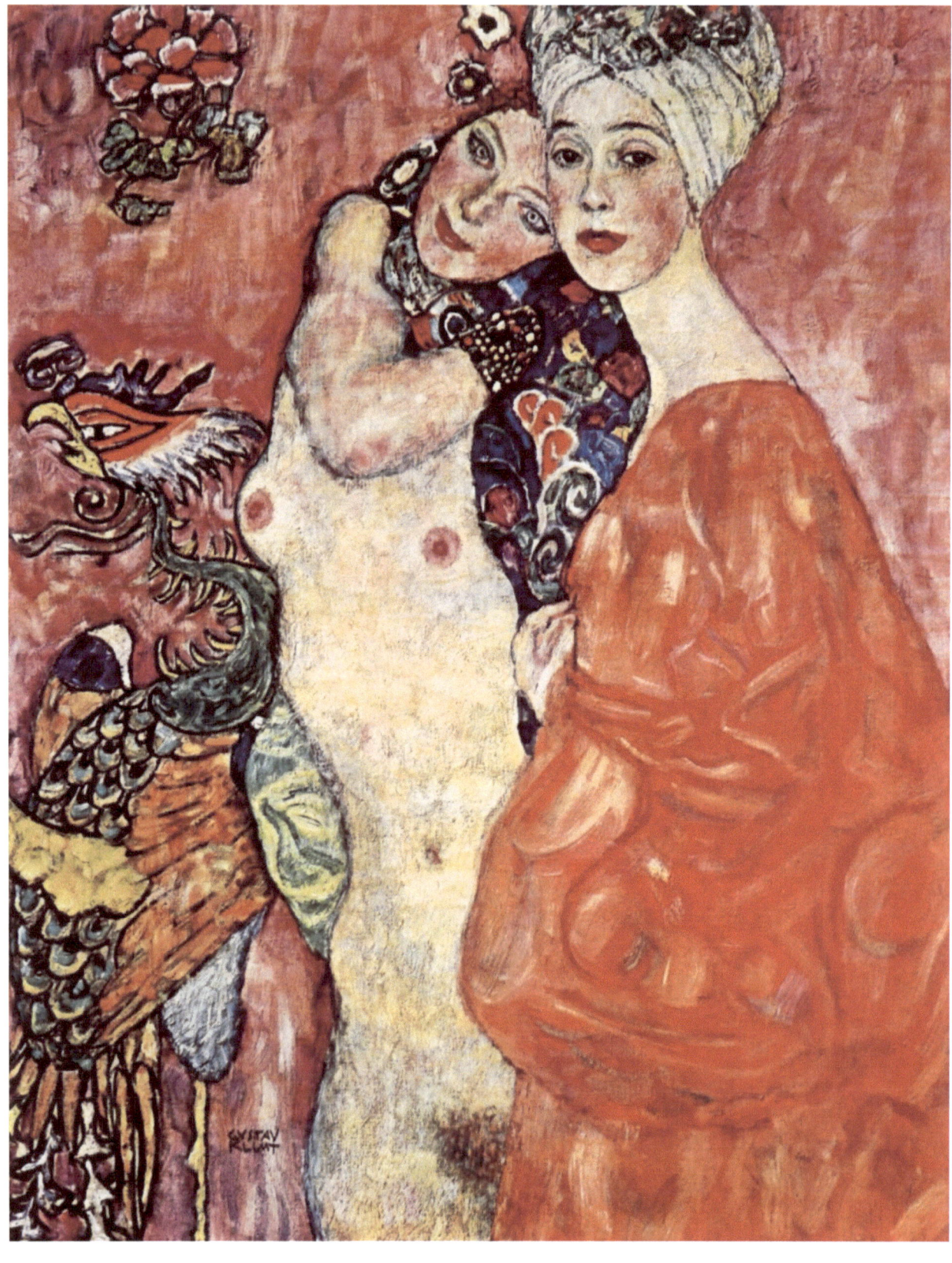

Nude Male Sitting

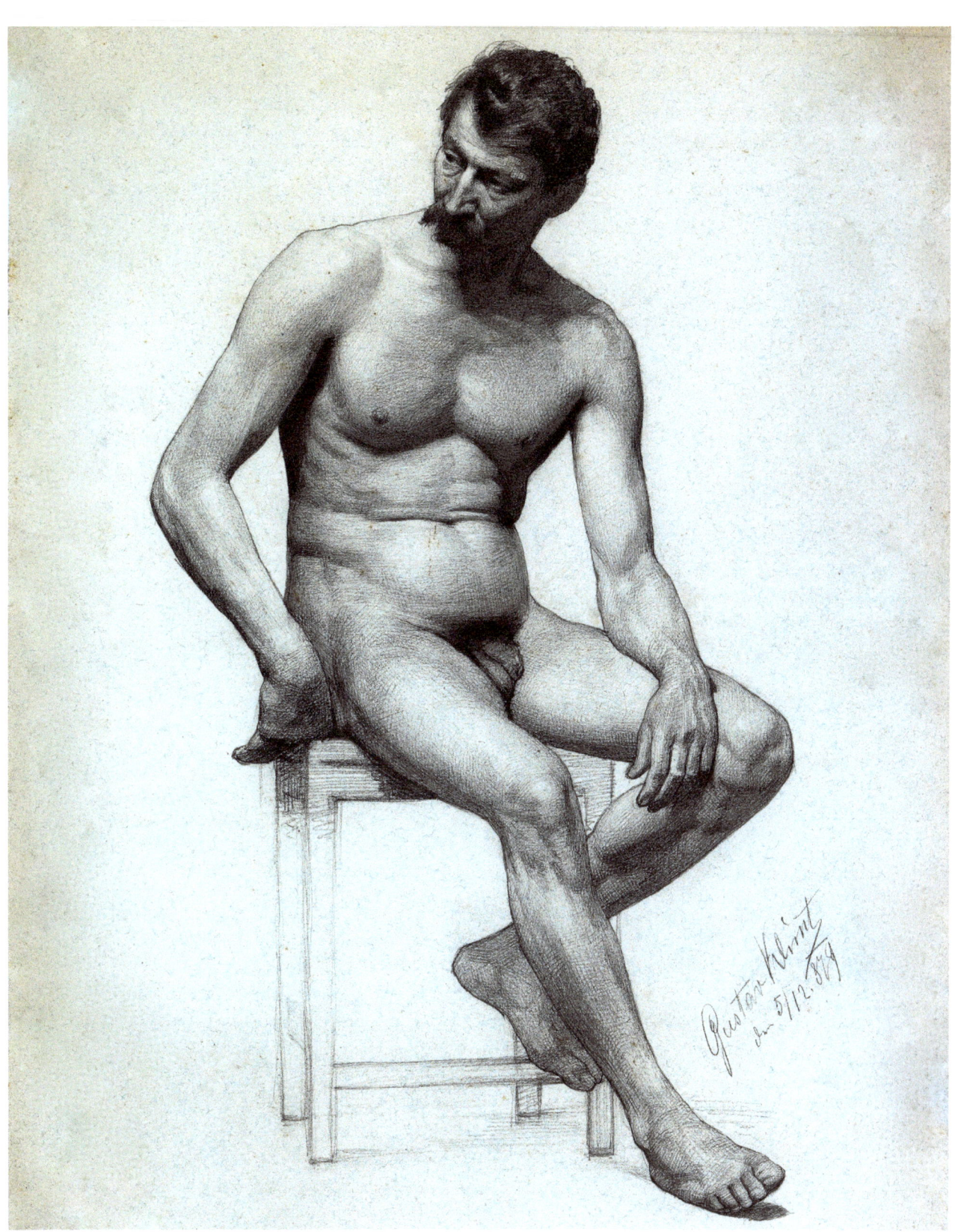

Judith

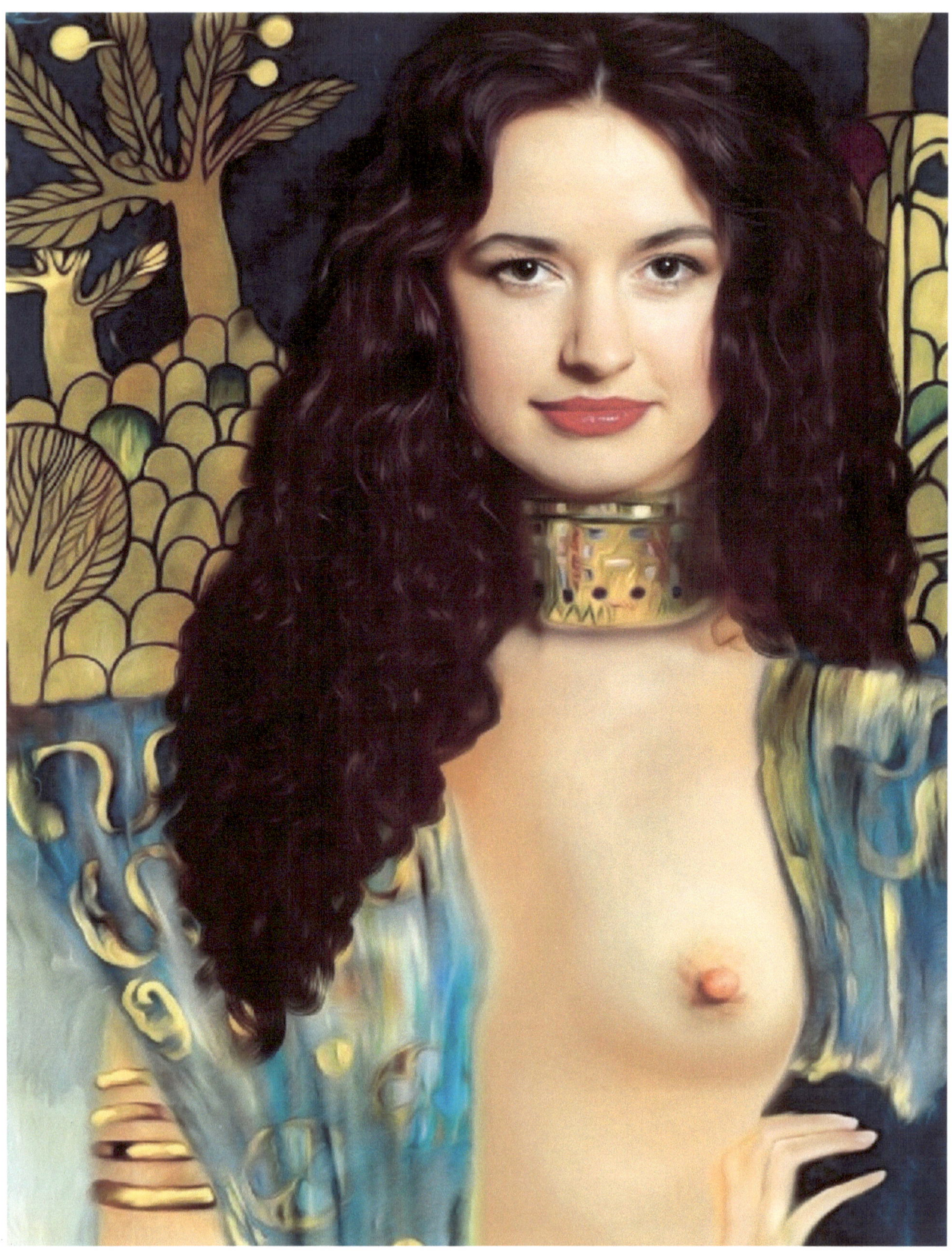

Danae

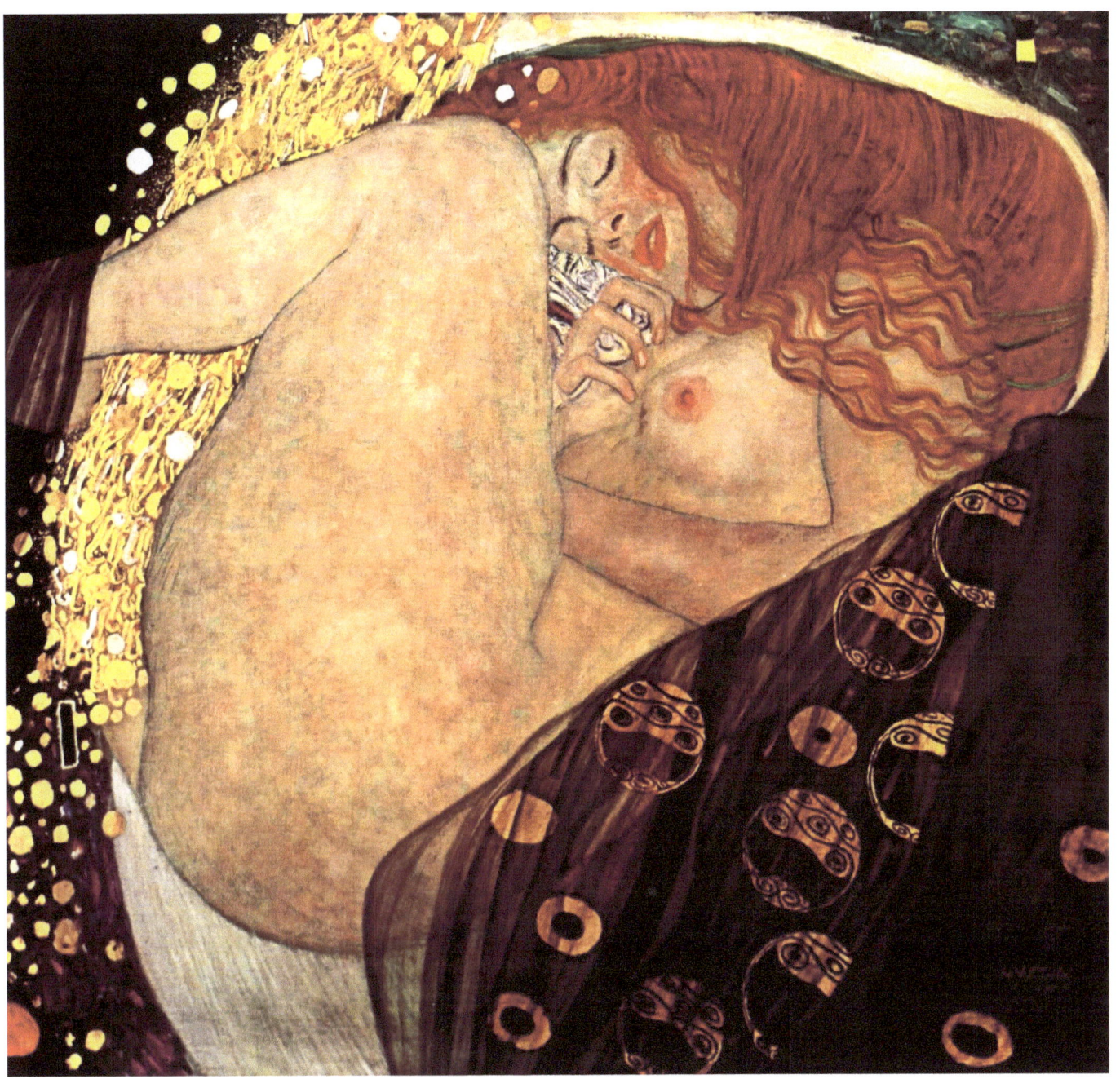

Cold Fish

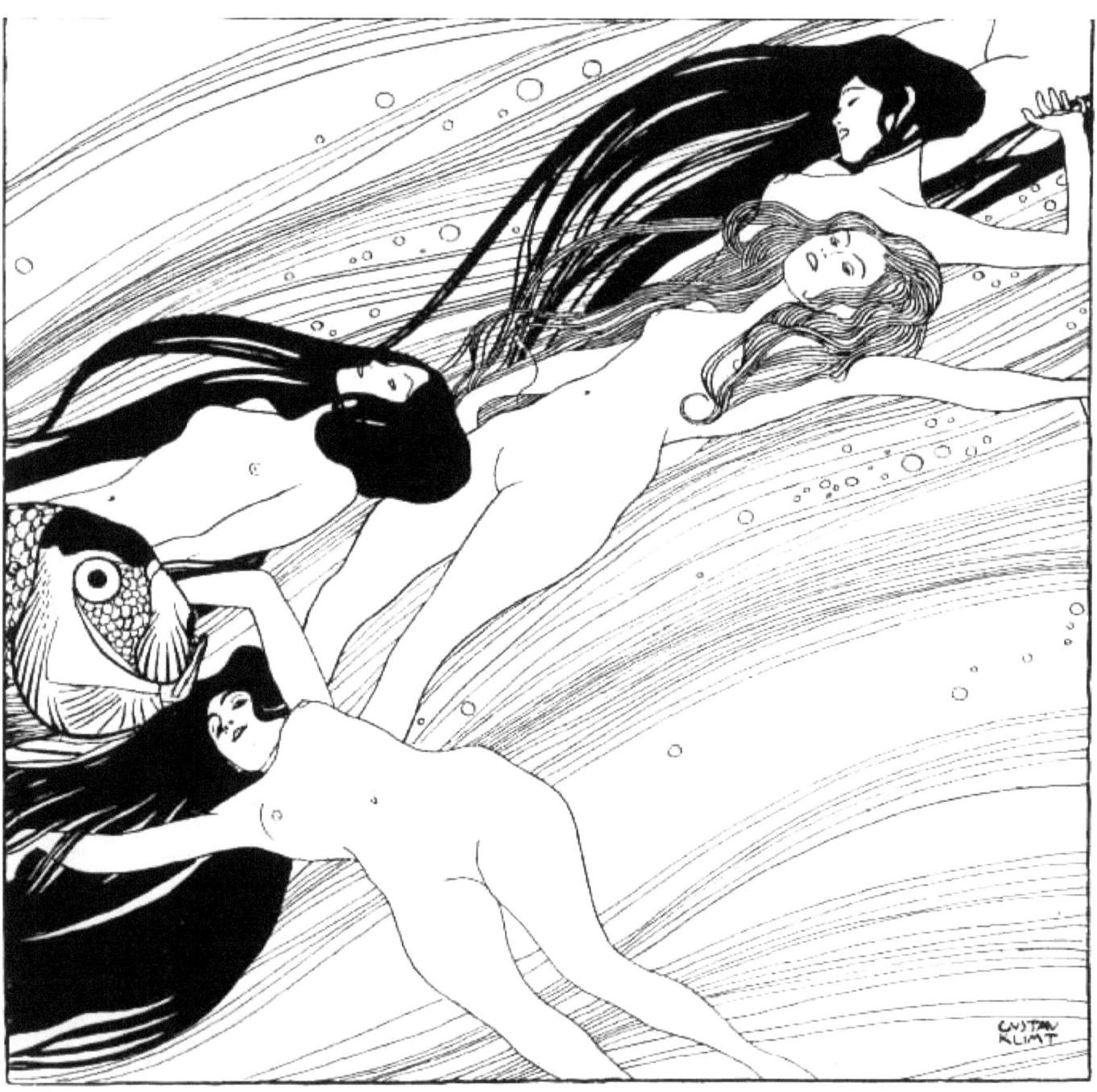

Fable

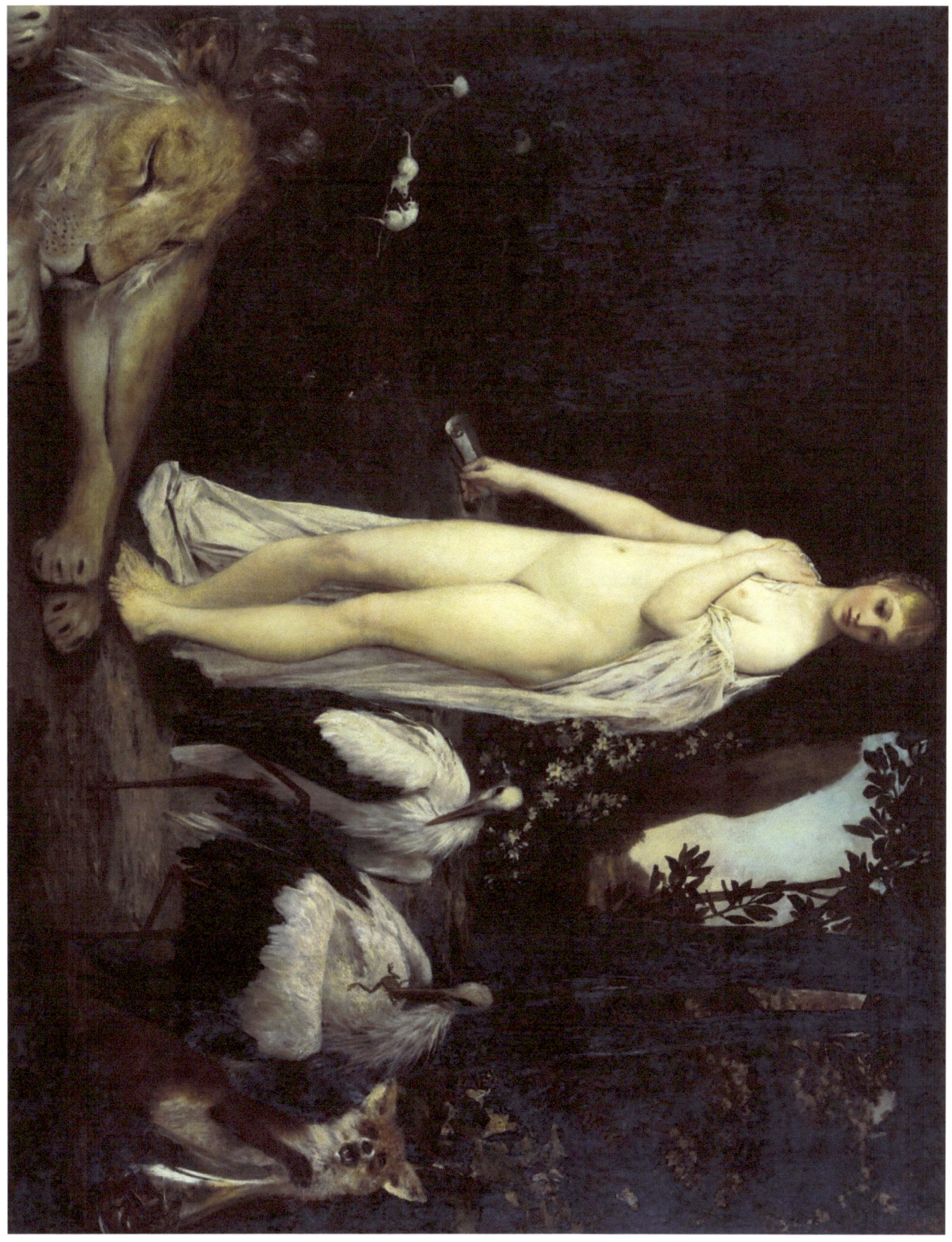

Death and Life

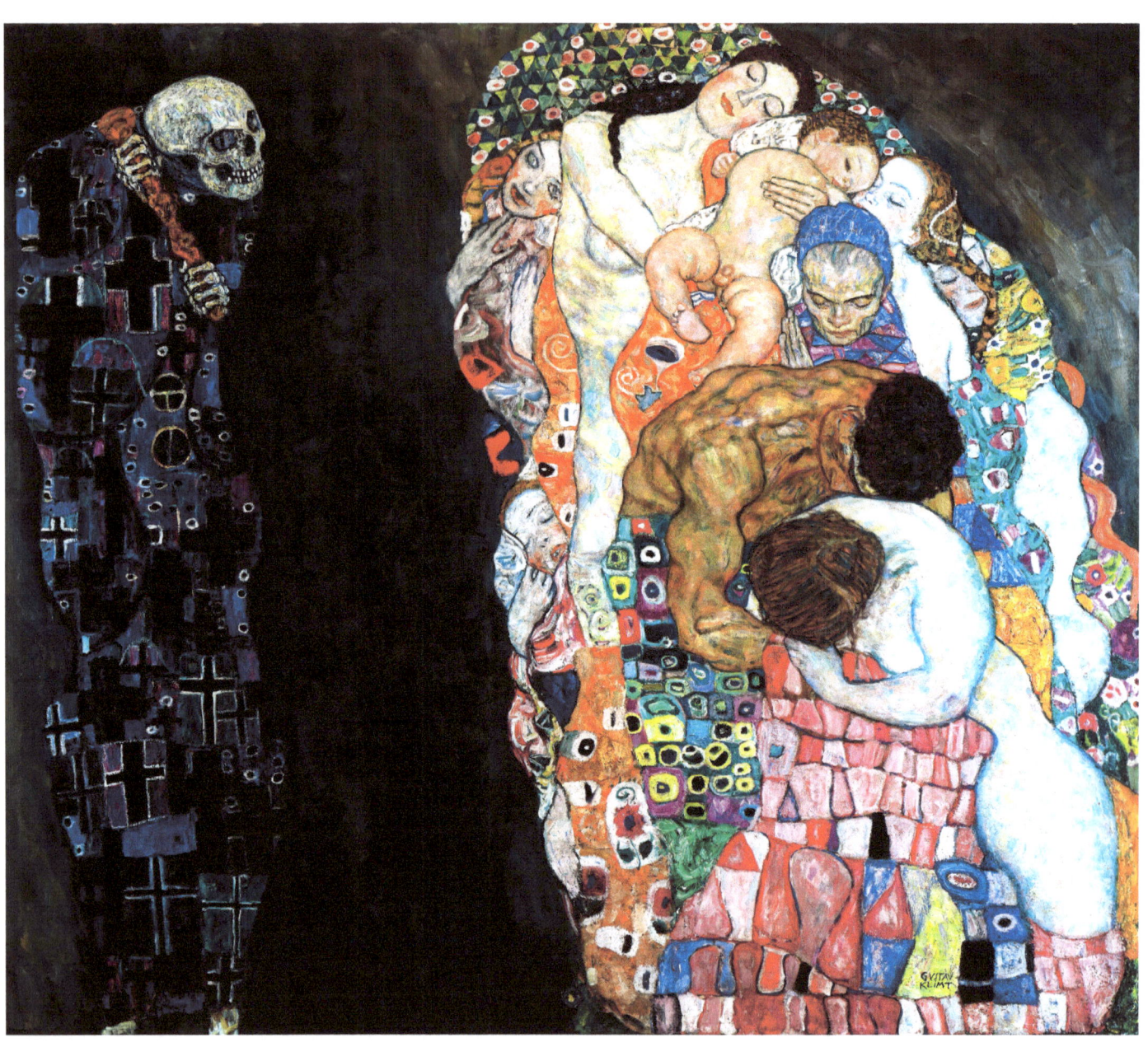

Nude Rear

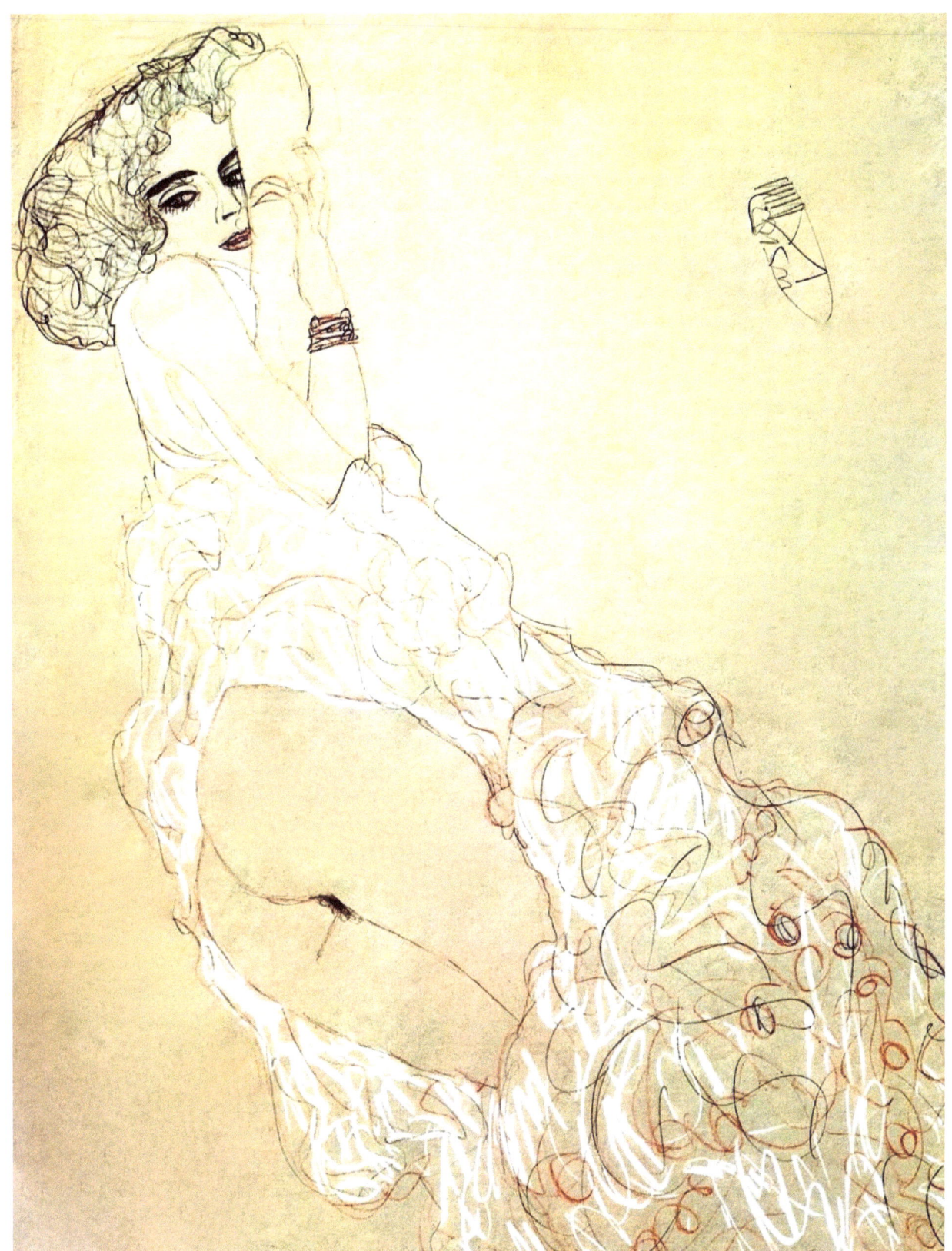

Girl With Blue Veil

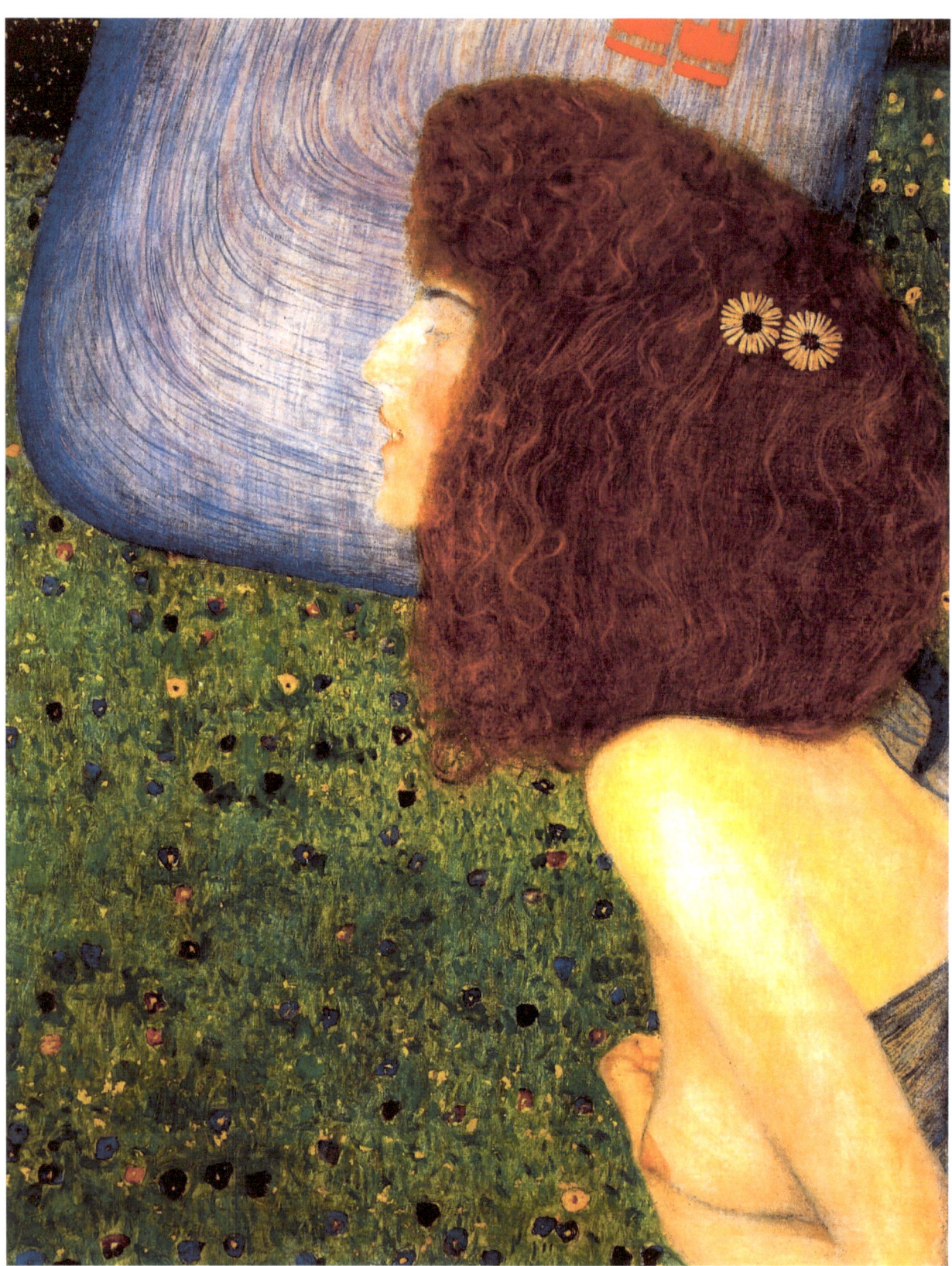

Suffering of the Weak

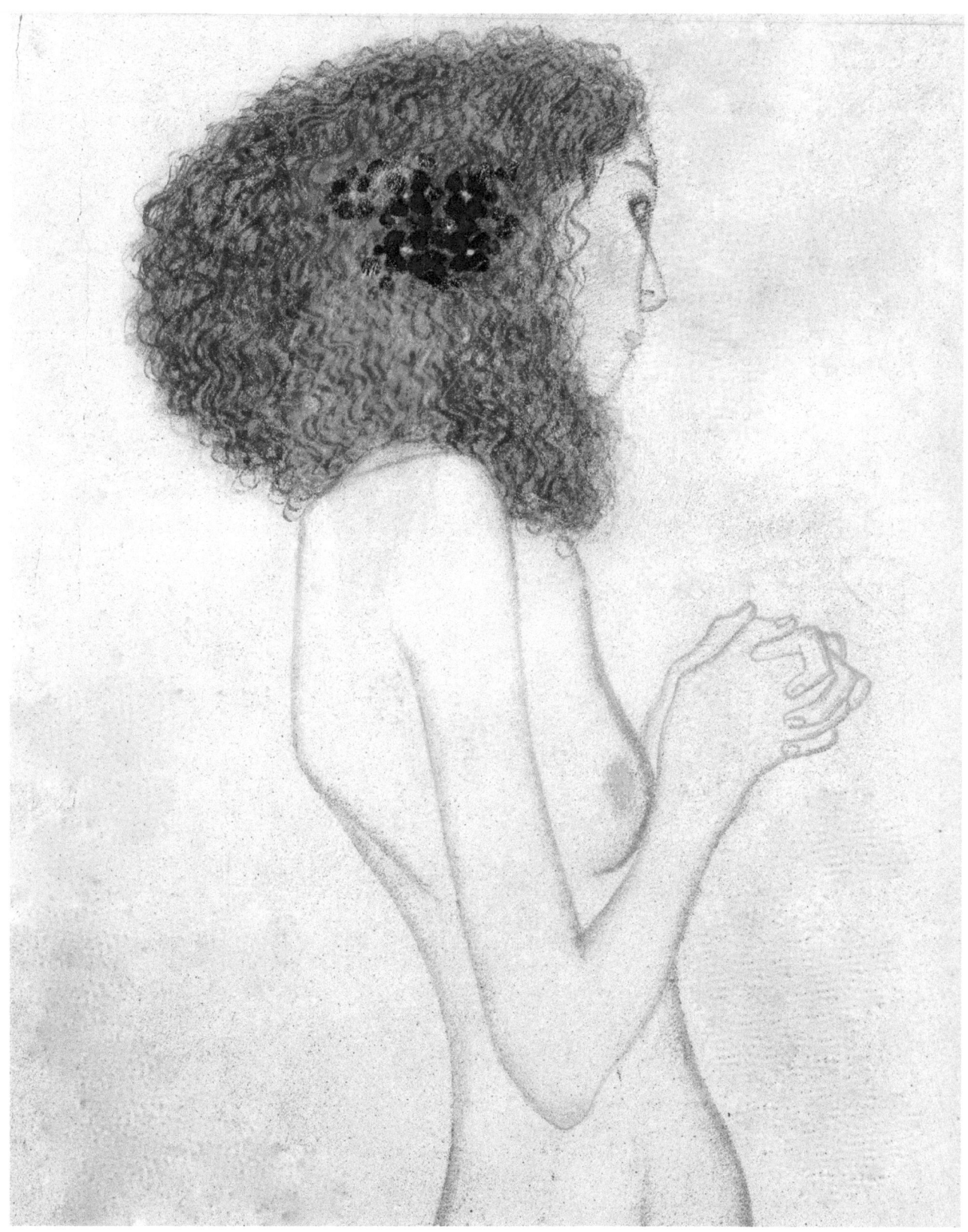

The Three Ages of Woman

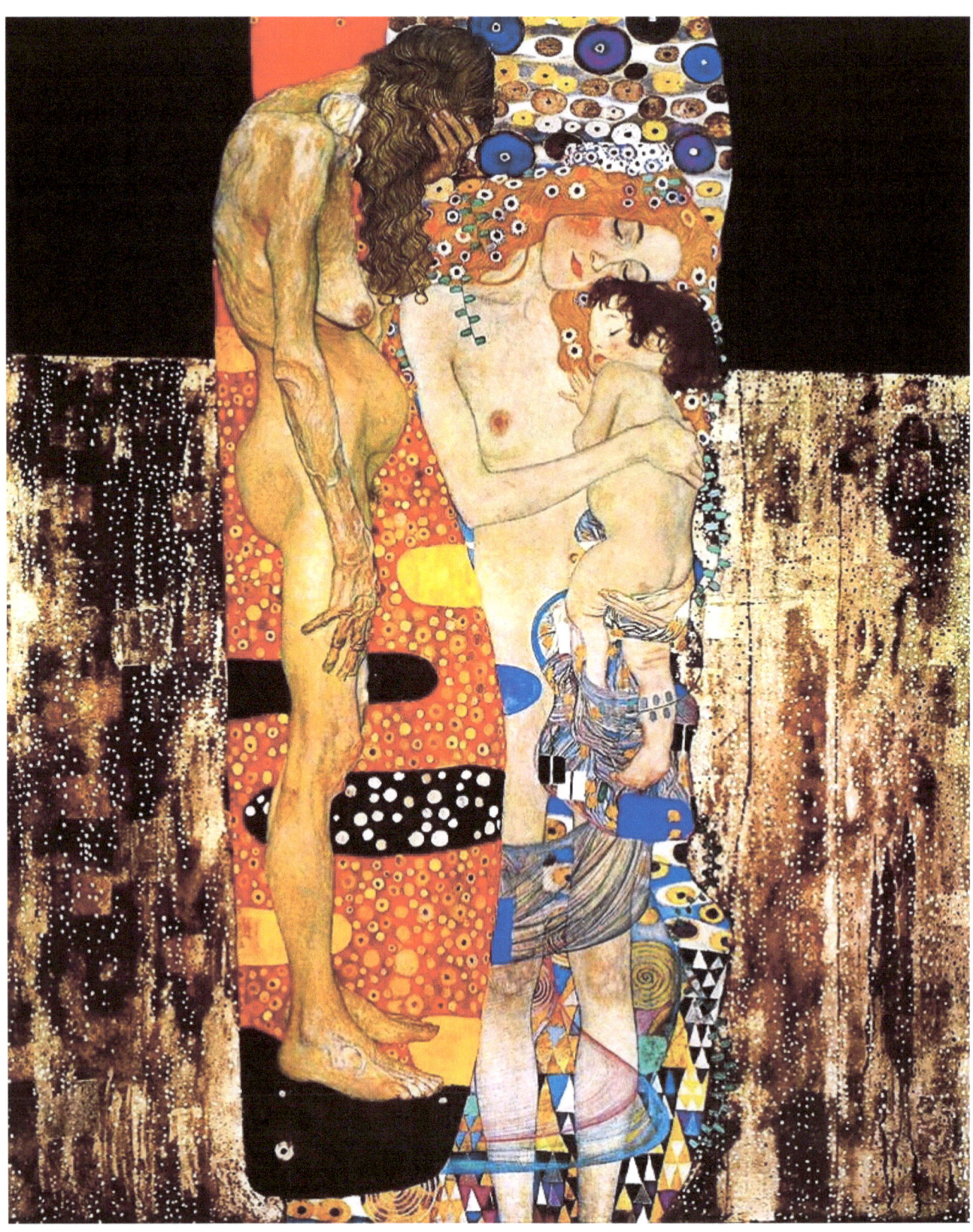

Female Nude Turned Left

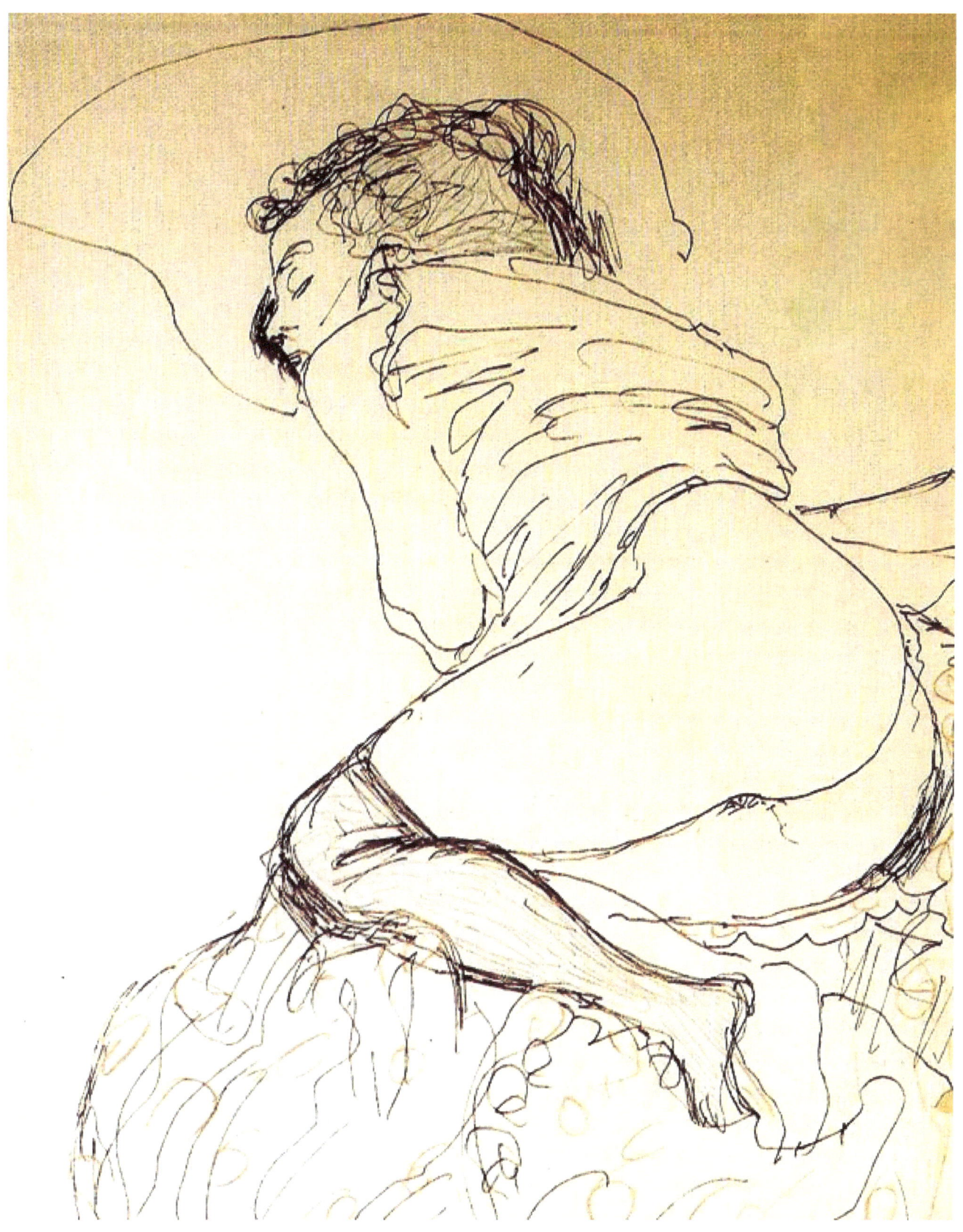

The Dancer

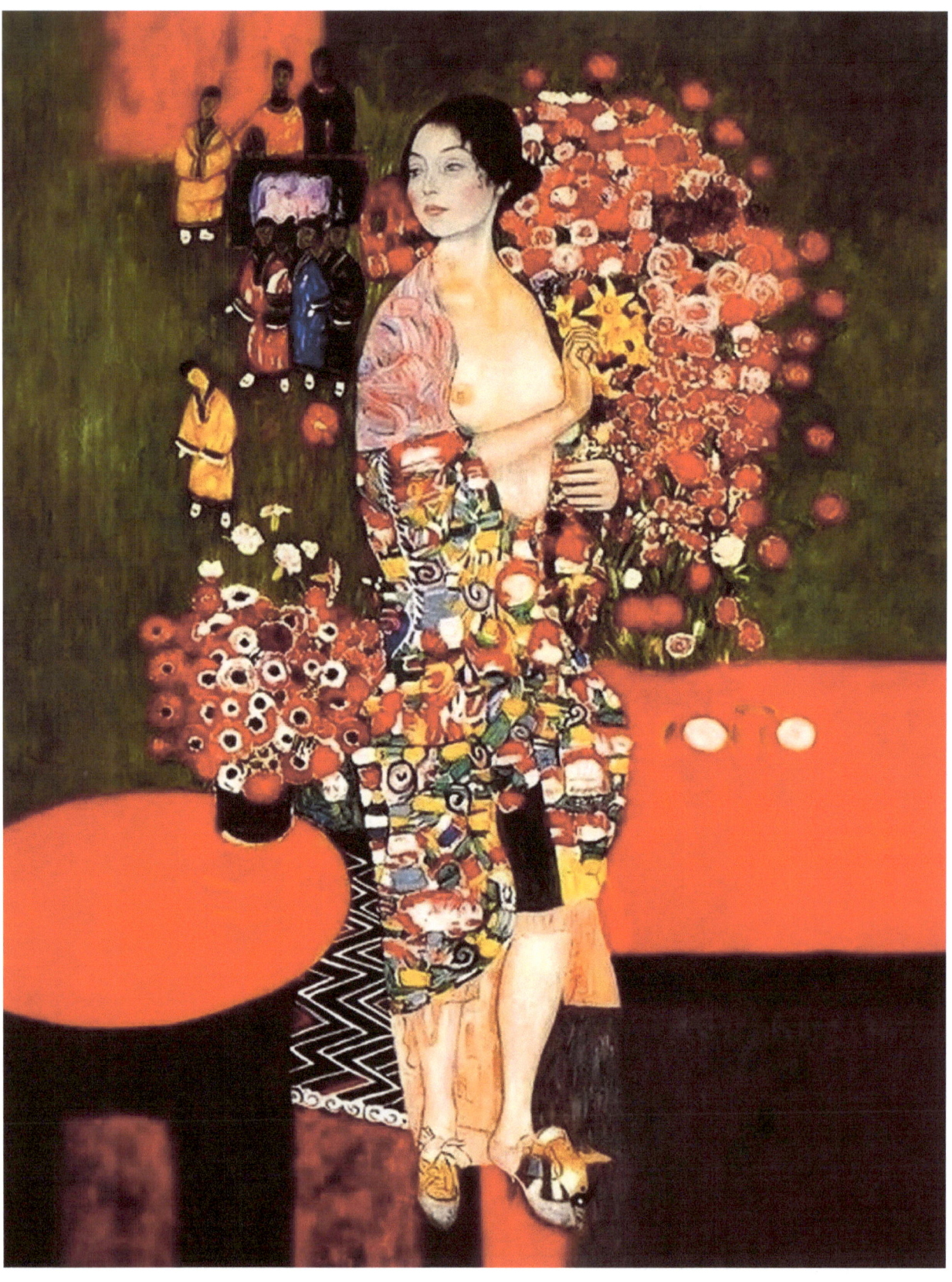

About the Author

The author currently resides in a small coastal town in Southern Oregon where he owns a small photography publishing business. He is also busy writing poetry and stories as well as working on his next book of themed art.

More Books by the Author

"Classic Fine Art Nudes: Volume One." This book features a collection of classic fine art nudes and is available on Amazon at https://www.amazon.com/Classic-Fine-Art-Nudes-One/dp/1093912073.

"Vintage Nudes of Yesteryear" presents sixty-five black and white photos of nude women produced generally between the years 1900 and 1923. It can be found on Amazon here: https://www.amazon.com/Vintage-Nudes-Yesteryear-Scott-Harker/dp/107044023X.

"Classic Fine Art Nudes: Volume Two." This book is the second book in a series collecting classic fine art nudes and is available on Amazon at https://www.amazon.com/Classic-Fine-Art-Nudes-Two/dp/1711917583.

"Classic Art of Absinthe" This book collects the best of the classic artwork about absinthe from the makers of absinthe, those who wanted absinthe banned and the artists of the time (mid-1800's to early 1900's). It is available on Amazon at https://www.amazon.com/Classic-Absinthe-Carl-Scott-Harker/dp/1653501189.

"Frankenstein's Monster in Oz" This book tells the story of how Frankenstein's Monster comes to Oz and what happens to him there. It is available on Amazon at https://www.amazon.com/Frankensteins-Monster-Carl-Scott-Harker/dp/1707291365.

"Am I Indigenous and Other Poems" – A collection of poems written between late 2016 and Autumn 2019. This book can be found on Amazon here: https://www.amazon.com/Am-I-Indigenous-Other-Poems/dp/1689862424.

"Poems By My Cat" – These poems reveal how cats view the world. The book can be found on Amazon here: https://www.amazon.com/Poems-Cat-Carl-Scott-Harker/dp/1793903239.

"100 Classic Poems to Read at Christmas Time" Here is a collection of some of the best Christmas poems written. The book can be found here: https://www.amazon.com/dp/B07J9YS7QK

"50 Great Poems to Read & Perform Out Loud" -This is a collection of the best poems ever written. The book can be found here: https://amzn.to/2zz8GFT.

"Seeds of Poetry: 21 Methods to Inspire Your Poetry and Other Creative Writings" – a book featuring tips with example about writing your own poetry You will find this book here: https://amzn.to/2HtMpO7.

"Exploring The Universe: The Art of Space" - Through the use of instruments such as the Hubble Space Telescope, scientists have captured the colorful art that space itself creates. This book collects some of the best of that space art. Here is the link: https://www.amazon.com/Exploring-Universe-Carl-Scott-Harker-ebook/dp/B077XQRPQL

www.ingramcontent.com/pod-product-compliance
Lightning Source LLC
Chambersburg PA
CBHW051212220526

45473CB00003B/1006